INK PAPER POLITICS

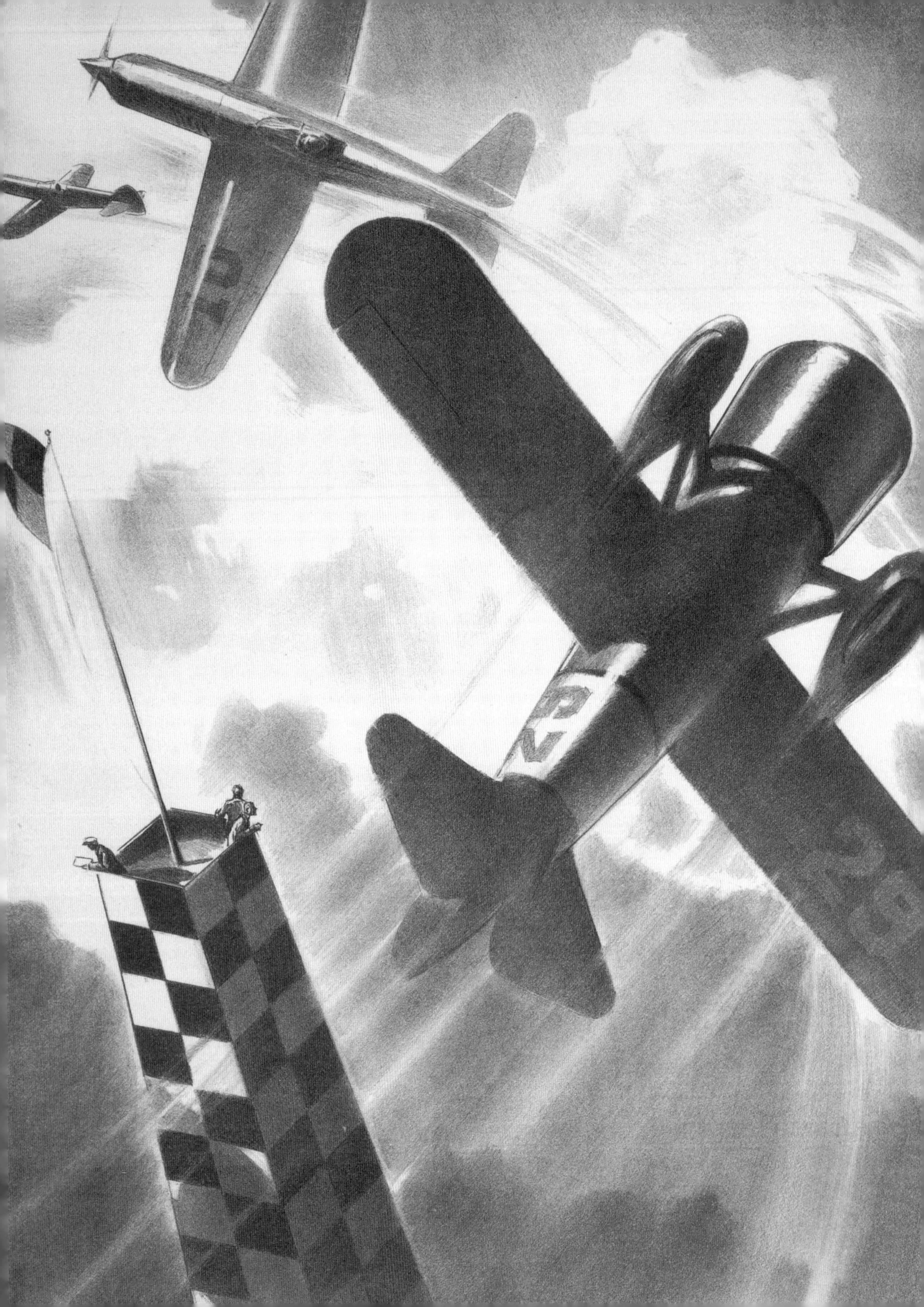

INK PAPER POLITICS

WPA-Era Printmaking from the Needles Collection

DPAM
DEPAUL ART MUSEUM

Ink, Paper, Politics: WPA-Era Printmaking from the Needles Collection
September 11–December 21, 2014
DePaul Art Museum
935 West Fullerton Avenue
Chicago, Illinois 60614

ISBN: 978-0-9789074-8-8

Distributed by the University of Chicago Press
www.press.uchicago.edu

Inside cover: cat. no. 48 (detail)
Frontispiece: cat. no. 29 (detail)

DPAM
DEPAUL ART MUSEUM

Contents

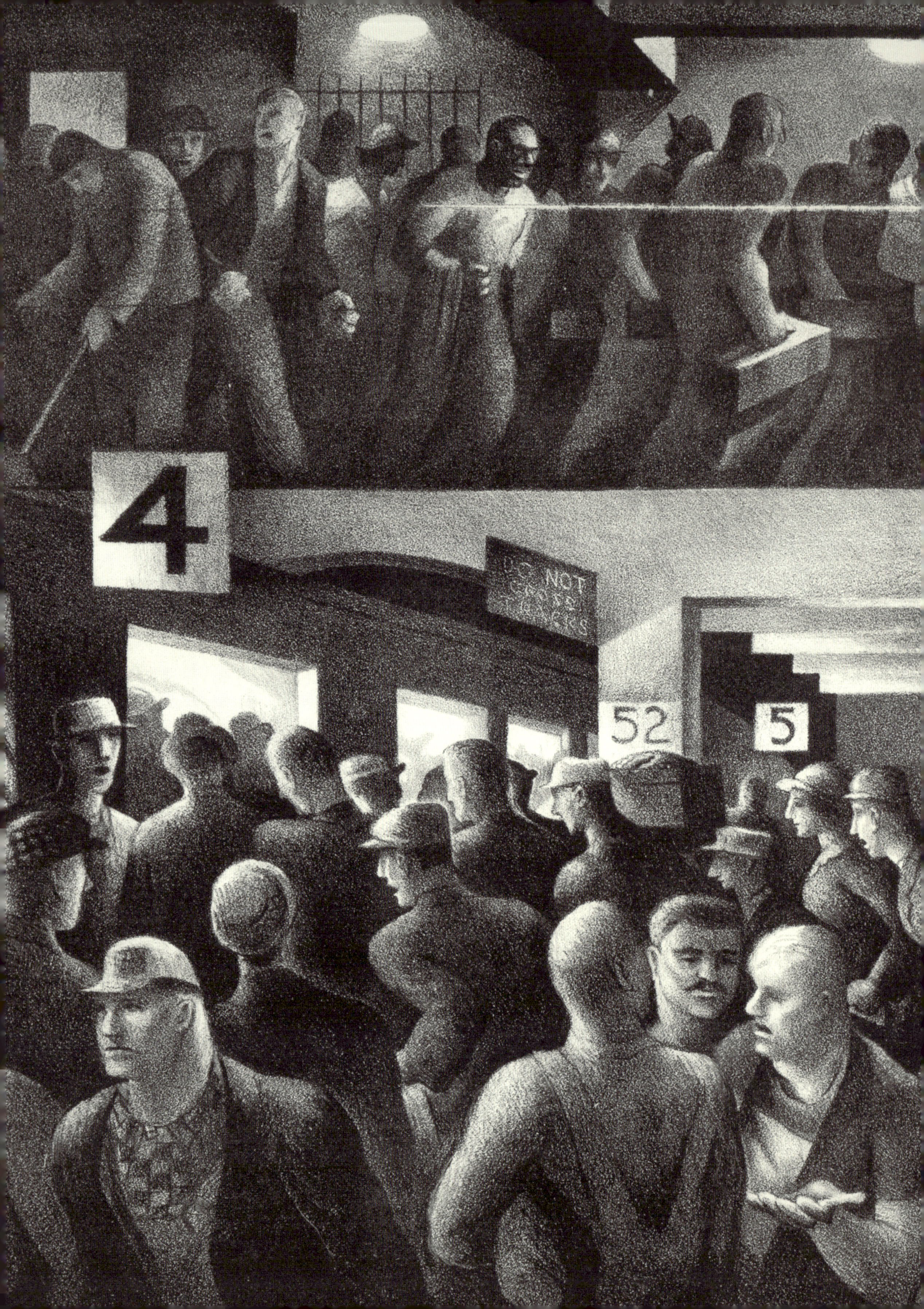
4
NOT
52
5

Introduction

Individually and together, Belverd Needles Jr. and Marian Powers Needles have had distinguished careers in the field of accounting, an area of study and practice they refer to as "the language of business." Both are teachers: he serves as EY Distinguished Professor of Accountancy at the Driehaus College of Business at DePaul University; she is Adjunct Professor and Academic Director of the Executive Education Programs at the Kellogg School of Management at Northwestern University. Jointly they have literally written the book on accounting—or, more accurately, a series of influential university textbooks for nascent accounting professionals. As their publications make clear, both Bel and Marian place great emphasis on the importance of an ethical foundation within the field. They believe that sound accounting practices are, among other things, a means of demonstrating the integrity and financial stability of corporations, institutions, and individuals. If accounting is indeed the language of business, they teach that it should be understandable, consistent, and clear. The same principles have led Bel and Marian to take active leadership roles in professional organizations at both national and international levels. They regularly travel widely in Europe, Asia, and the Middle East to teach and to present their research, and to provide consultation for public and private entities.

Quite apart from their demanding and hectic professional lives, Bel and Marian have also built a serious and ambitious collection of fine-art prints, ranging from Old Masters to work by contemporary artists. Over the course of thirty years, they have become connoisseurs, well versed in several key areas in the history of printmaking. Works from their collection are regularly included in exhibitions at major museums, and they have themselves undertaken a series of publications to make their holdings more widely available. At first glance, there is very little connection between their collecting and professional careers—and deliberately so. They began their collection precisely to give themselves an area of interest unrelated to accounting. They have clearly enjoyed the opportunity to take part in a different world: gaining expertise in the physical characteristics of prints; meeting dealers, experts, and other collectors; and incorporating museum visits into their wide travels.

And yet, as Bel's preface in this volume attests, there is common ground between these seemingly disparate worlds. Bel and Marian have been remarkably disciplined in focusing on their areas of interest, avoiding the temptation to collect broadly. As they expanded their knowledge of prints and artists, they also systematized their acquisitions, developing criteria on which to judge artists, eras, and individual prints. They set and achieved goals in their collection, upgraded when opportunities were presented, and brought a set of professional skills to a field that often operates on emotional and subjective responses. Their scrupulous record-keeping and collection management—while not unique—are notable.

Their collecting practices, however, diverge with their professional values in one key way. It would be easy to imagine that an accounting mindset would incline a collector to think of objects as assets or investments, and encourage active trading in the market. But for Bel and Marian, this is not the case. They literally live with their collection; they are surrounded in their home by a rotating series of installations, linked to artists or themes they choose. Beyond their own enjoyment of the collection, the Needleses are eager to share their works with like-minded students, friends, and collectors, encouraging the kind of patient looking that prints can reward so richly. In that spirit, Bel and Marian have made a generous gift to the DePaul Art Museum: one hundred prints made during the era of the Great Depression, when—among many other relief programs—the federal government directed support to artists under the auspices of the Works Progress Administration (WPA). The present catalogue, and the exhibition it accompanies, celebrates this extraordinary gift.

The story of WPA support for the arts deserves retelling, in part because it resonates with current debates about government spending and economic recovery. Conceived as an experiment in 1934 and managed at the state level, the WPA essentially paid artists to produce work. WPA programs were controversial from the start, their "make-work" format supposedly fostering low standards of skill and efficiency. Then as now, art projects were particularly vulnerable to satire and political critique, and the WPA was reshaped repeatedly over its nine years of existence to address concerns over eligibility, reporting requirements, artistic quality, and politics. WPA funds supported thousands of artists working in a range of artistic media—from murals in public buildings to easel paintings and poster design. Also notable is the number of women and minority artists who participated in the WPA.

Printmaking supported by the WPA is a particularly interesting area of study: the design of the program itself, the political climate, and the very nature of the medium together produced a distinctive approach to style and subject matter, impressive technical innovations, and a surprising degree of social fluidity among artists. Administering printmaking was complicated by the need for space and equipment, a problem the WPA solved by establishing regional workshops in which artists shared work space and press time. This had the serendipitous effect of bringing together artists who might never have crossed paths otherwise, building connections across lines of race, class, and gender.

WPA administrators believed printmaking was the most "democratic" medium because it was inexpensive, nonexclusive, and worked well for narrative or didactic purposes. That premise was widely accepted among the artists who participated in the WPA, and in fact many prints of the era demonstrate strong commonalities in style and subject matter: they celebrate labor and industry, advocate on behalf of the poor, and critique wealth and greed. Within the WPA, recognizable subject matter and narrative content were the norm. Abstraction, while known and widely discussed in the 1930s, seldom appeared in WPA projects, though many WPA artists went on to fame in later decades, and some, like Jackson Pollock and Stuart Davis, came to be known for their avant-garde work. This preference for representation dominated printmaking in particular, perhaps reflecting assumptions about the taste of general audiences, the didactic and political purposes of government-sponsored art, or even the gratitude of artists for the program that enabled them to continue their work. Moreover, that tilt toward content exerted a gravitational pull in American art that reached beyond its origin in WPA projects.

Typical WPA prints—socially engaged and rich in detail—relate to a variety of academic disciplines, from gender studies to the history of technology, making them particularly valuable as primary documents for teaching. In addition, the direct treatment of issues of social justice in WPA-era art makes the Needles collection a significant and relevant contribution to the DePaul Art Museum and an appropriate reflection of the university's values and culture. Without question, Bel and Marian's generous gift will bring knowledge and pleasure to generations of students, scholars, and visitors to the museum.

Many people facilitated this project over several years. Particular gratitude goes to Andrea Jones, formerly the collection manager for the Needles collection, and her successor, Makenzi Fricker. The museum's student interns, Nik Massey and Amy Kellenberger, took on important parts of the preparation, including photography and framing. Laura Fatemi, associate director of the museum, designed the exhibition with care and finesse; Alison Kleiman designed the installation graphics and handled countless administrative details; and Gregory Harris provided assistance with curatorial and installation issues. Elizabeth Seaton, curator at the Beach Museum in Lawrence, Kansas, generously drew on her expertise and knowledge of the collection to provide crucial advice. Helen Langa, associate professor of art history at American University, provided an insightful view of the culture and politics of the WPA for this catalogue, and we are enormously grateful for her scholarly contribution. We thank the Terra Foundation for American Art and the Foundation's board member Chet Gougis for their donation in support of this publication. Finally, our deepest gratitude goes to Belverd Needles Jr. and Marian Powers Needles for their interest in and support for the museum over many years, and for their extraordinarily generous gift.

Louise Lincoln
Director

Collectors' Foreword

Belverd E. Needles Jr. and Marian Powers Needles

We began collecting prints almost forty years ago, when we purchased *Ten Pound Hammer* by the American artist Thomas Hart Benton in a small gallery in Lubbock, Texas. Shortly thereafter, we responded to an advertisement in the *Saturday Review* and received a mailing from Associated American Artists (AAA) in New York. Founded by Reeves Lewenthal in the 1930s, AAA specialized in making prints by well-known and not-so-well-known artists available to the general public at affordable prices. The company was able to do this by issuing large editions of 250 impressions. Typically in the 1930s, AAA prints were sold by mail and in department stores for five dollars. Some of these prints, such as those by Grant Wood and Benton, became very valuable; they make up a significant part of our collection of Regionalist prints. After Sylvan Cole became the director of AAA, the company sold annual editions of slightly more expensive prints by catalogue, such as those by Will Barnet. We made a practice of purchasing a selection of these prints from AAA each year, including a complete suite by Robert Kipness one year.

Eventually, we made it to New York and met Mr. Cole; later we also met the next director of AAA, Robert Conway, and his assistant, Susan Teller, both of whom became lifelong friends and were very influential in the development of our collection. As our collecting of American prints became more informed and focused, we decided to concentrate on those from the one-hundred-year period of 1860 to 1960. Our desire was to form a strong collection representing all types of American print-making from this period.

The question of why we chose to collect prints often arises from friends and others. Our reasons are practical, intellectual, and aesthetic. We prefer to collect fine prints rather than other kinds of art for several reasons. First, it is difficult to collect paintings or drawings by well-known artists from early time periods because most of those that are worth collecting are either in museums or are quite expensive—too expensive for the young college professors we were when we began collecting. The very rare work that is available and inexpensive enough for an ordinary person to collect is often of lesser quality or by an unrecognized artist. Since we were not satisfied to collect lesser works by great artists or works by secondary artists, our only real option was to collect prints.

Prints are original works of art—even though they are created in multiple impressions—because the original plate or block from which the print is made is prepared (and usually printed) by the artist. Additionally, artists commonly sign their prints. It is important to determine that an impression was made during the artist's lifetime.

Our second reason for collecting prints—as opposed to drawings—was a matter of personal taste. Drawings are often sketches or preliminary studies for other projects, while prints are usually finished compositions that represent the artist's fully realized vision of a subject. To our eye, this is a desirable characteristic of prints.

A third reason for collecting prints is the connection they provide to the artists who made them and the lives that they led. As wonderful as a Mozart sonata is, we cannot actually hear Mozart play. The work has to be interpreted by someone else. However, with fine prints, we can see the particular work that the artist made. Prints are very personal statements, often reflecting an artist's most intimate feelings and concerns.

After deciding to collect prints, choosing which prints we would collect was the next step. Our focus is on prints of the highest quality that contribute to the goals of our collection, creating a cohesive whole. To achieve this goal, we defined six criteria by which to judge potential additions to our collection: the importance of the artist, the importance of the work in the artist's oeuvre, rarity, impression, condition, and intangibles.

To determine an artist's eligibility for inclusion in our collection, we first decided what constitutes an American artist. For the purposes of our collection, we identify American artists as those who have American citizenship or have spent a significant portion of their careers in the United States. Thus, James McNeill Whistler, an American who spent most of his life in England, is included, as are immigrants who produced prints after they arrived in the United States. Further, a significant portion of the artist's print oeuvre needs to have been made prior to 1960.

We further divide artists into four categories. A Category I artist is a major artist who had significant importance and influence in the history of American printmaking before 1960, a major body of print work, many images in important collections of American prints, and images that must be included in any major survey of American printmaking. The key difference between Category I and Category II artists is the artist's influence in the history of American printmaking prior to 1960. Thus, Category II artists have a significant body of work that includes important contributions—but is of secondary influence—to the history of American printmaking before 1960, noteworthy innovations in a segment of American printmaking, some images that would be included in important collections of American prints, and images that would likely be included in any major survey of American printmaking before 1960 that went beyond top artists. About forty of the artists featured in this exhibition are what we define as Category I or II artists.

Generally speaking, Category II artists have a larger body of significant work and a broader influence in the history of American printmaking before 1960 than Category III artists. Category III artists contributed to a particular segment of the history of printmaking before 1960, creating one or more striking images that could be included in an important collection of American prints and images that would likely be included in a survey of a particular area of printmaking. Finally, a Category IV artist is a printmaker who is a member of a particular group of American printmakers from before 1960, has one or more images that are representative of that group of artists, and has images that might be included in a survey of that group.

We are particularly interested in the intellectual and historical ties between artists and their work. Every print has a story to tell if you take the time to find out what it is. This back story is especially strong in prints from the Works Progress Administration (WPA) era, when the country was experiencing its worst depression, leftist and communist viewpoints were especially prevalent among artists, and the government (through the WPA) served as an important impetus to art-making. Many of the artists working in this period were not well known and would be categorized as Category III or IV artists. Nevertheless, they created interesting images of high quality that are representative of the period. Some images from the artists in these categories are among our favorites.

Our second criterion for collecting a print is its importance in the artist's oeuvre. We look for prints that are recognizable as by an artist's hand and, through their technique and subject, represent the best work of the artist. For example, a strong work from the artist's mature period is favored. For Category I or II artists, we like to include interesting works from early or post-mature periods, but we do not collect unimportant or atypical works by these artists.

We also consider the criteria of rarity, impression, and condition. We favor small editions or rare works over larger editions if our first two collection criteria are met. The print must be a very fine or fine lifetime impression in excellent or very good condition. Finally, there are the intangible factors. From an emotional standpoint, the image must "speak" to us. A good measure of this last criterion is that the image is one that we never tire of examining and searching for meaning. Since works of this nature are quite rare and often too expensive for our budget, such collecting requires patience and is something of a scavenger hunt. By adding a few prints each year, we have created a collection that serves as a fulsome representation of the century of American printmaking from 1860 to 1960, as well as bringing us great joy.

Because we both are accounting academics, doing research and coauthoring works together, we wanted to become involved in a community outside our professional field. Collecting prints has enabled us to meet this objective and, in the process, develop many friendships. If we tried to list all those friends who have enriched our collecting experience, we would undoubtedly leave out many important ones. In addition to Robert Conway and Susan Teller (mentioned earlier), we must discuss two others whose influence has been essential. At the first Chicago Print Fair we attended, we met Maury Alberti at one of the booths and immediately became fast friends. Maury was a successful

Chicago dentist but, like us, loved prints. After collecting for many years, upon his retirement, he started his own business as a private print dealer specializing in American prints from the exact period we were interested in: 1860–1960. We miss the many good meals and discussions of American prints we had with Maury, who sadly passed away.

In the early 1970s, we visited R. S. Johnson Fine Art on Michigan Avenue in Chicago. R. Stanley Johnson spent an hour showing us the differences in various states of Rembrandt etchings. This touched off a period of study and subsequent returns to the gallery, as well as visits to art museums, including the Prints and Drawings Department at the Art Institute of Chicago. We also developed a close friendship with Ursula and Stanley Johnson.

We have always wanted our collection to be used for education. Over the years, we have organized exhibitions at DePaul and other universities around the country. We are pleased to work with the DePaul Art Museum on this exhibition and delighted that these prints will enter the museum's permanent collection for future study by students and faculty at the university.

Printmaking, Artistic Diversity, and Cultural Democracy in 1930s America

Helen Langa

The history of printmaking as a significant form of fine art in the United States begins well before the 1930s. However, the flourishing of artist printmakers during the era of the Great Depression and the New Deal—a period of economic and political uncertainty during which Americans sought to understand themselves, their country, and their culture in new ways—was somewhat unexpected. The efflorescence of interest in etchings, lithographs, and silkscreen prints during the late 1930s and early 1940s—evidenced so strongly in the works from the Needles collection in this exhibition—drew on several decades of efforts by individual artists, organized print societies, gallery owners, nonprofit arts organizations, and commercial marketers to enhance appreciation for prints among art collectors and the larger public.[1]

This growing interest in printmaking provided a foundation for its surprising success at the Graphic Arts Division of the Works Progress Administration's Federal Art Project (WPA-FAP), which was established in late 1935 and closed in 1943. Employment on the WPA-FAP allowed artists to survive the Depression, gain technical skills, share aesthetic interests, and show their work to the public without competing for gallery representation. Many excellent prints in diverse media were created for the Graphic Arts Division, though many continued to be produced by artists working independently and in regional groups.

The expanded interest in lithographic prints in the 1930s was also indebted to numerous skilled printers—in business for themselves or working for the FAP—who assisted artists in editioning their lithographic images. Histories of American printmaking during this period tend to emphasize either the WPA-FAP's successes or those of independent artists and organizations, but a full understanding of the period requires that both groups be seen as contributing to the increased vitality of printmaking across the country.

Well before the Depression, American cultural critics began to emphasize the importance of claiming a specific national and democratic heritage in the arts, and to reject the dominance of European aesthetic and cultural models. In a 1924 article, artist Benton Spruance noted that printmakers were producing "an American art that is art and an American art that is American."[2] By 1942 art dealer Carl Zigrosser could assert that American graphic arts had been transformed "from provincialism to the beginnings of a national school."[3] Spruance, Zigrosser, Holger Cahill (director of the FAP), and other promoters of printmaking as a form of art that suited the values of a democratic society shared the view, derived from Walt Whitman, that the American nation required "a program of culture, drawn out, not for a single class alone, or for the parlors or the lecture rooms, but with an eye to practical life."[4] This emphasis on forms of culture accessible to all citizens, an ideal often referred to as "cultural democracy," helped to raise the status of printmaking as an art form, one which seemed particularly likely to interest a new generation of American viewers and art collectors. While such a concept was more rhetorical than literal—considering that print editions of twenty-five to two hundred impressions were only minimally accessible compared to such mass-produced forms of popular culture as comic books—it allowed both artists and cultural analysts to frame the multiple-original status of prints as a significant shift away from the elitism associated with painting and sculpture.

It took some time to develop this perspective. During the first two decades of the twentieth century, various artists and organizations sought to promote prints as interesting and aesthetically vigorous forms of art, building on the popularity of the late-nineteenth-century Etching Revival. Beginning in the 1880s, a number of American artists found it lucrative to travel to Europe and even further abroad to record views of foreign architectural monuments and picturesque landscapes. Intaglio prints—including drypoints, etchings, and aquatints—were typically produced in small editions and sold to print connoisseurs in the United States, where they were appreciated as demonstrating both a nuanced artistic touch and skillful technique. Etchings and wood engravings were also valued as book and advertising illustrations, and numerous artists supported their independent fine-art careers through commercial commissions. In the early 1900s in California, a distinctive school of color woodblock and linoleum-cut landscape prints—influenced by Arthur Wesley Dow's teaching and the work of three sisters, Frances, May, and Edna Gearhart—emerged.[5] These works, because they were hand-printed in relatively small editions (twenty to thirty impressions with some individual color variation), were also considered pleasing objects for elite connoisseurship.

Etching clubs and print societies were eventually organized in almost every state, often centered in larger cities such as Brooklyn, Chicago, Honolulu, and Minneapolis. The California Society of Etchers was founded in 1912, and the Brooklyn Society of Etchers in 1914; by the early 1940s, there were numerous media-inclusive regional groups, such as the Prairie Printmakers in Kansas and the Lone Star Printmakers in Texas.[6] The members of these groups ranged from ambitious amateurs to professional artists; their repertoire of subjects gradually expanded to include American regional landscapes and cityscapes, a few abstractions or fanciful aestheticized themes, and diverse images drawn from observed social experience. Urban artists showed their works at galleries and museums, while artists outside major cities gained visibility at state fair art shows. Anyone could submit work to juried national exhibitions.[7] In 1931 the Brooklyn Society of Etchers was reorganized as the Society of American Etchers, a national organization that played a significant role in promoting interest in fine-art prints under the leadership of esteemed intaglio printmaker John Taylor Arms.[8] However, not until 1947 did it change its name to include other print media and, a few years later, become the Society of American Graphic Artists. The American Institute of Graphic Arts (AIGA), also founded in 1914, was predominantly devoted to encouraging fine commercial design, but beginning in 1925–26, it underwrote an annual traveling exhibition entitled *Fifty Best Prints*, whose participants were determined by an AIGA-appointed jury. These developments highlight the growing importance of printmaking as an art form from the 1910s to the 1940s, one that was supported by a diverse and growing array of national and regional organizations.

The dominance of intaglio printing was challenged in the 1910s, with the rising interest in lithography as a fine art rather than a commercial printmaking process. Artists interested in exploring more modernist subjects were increasingly drawn to lithography, while the delicacy and precision of etching continued to be exploited by artists interested in both conservative and more contemporary themes. While etchings or woodcuts could be developed individually in the artist's studio, the technical challenges of lithography originally made it less easily accessible to those not committed to a printmaking practice. However, this began to change after George Miller and Bolton Brown set up lithographic press shops in New York in 1917 and 1918 (respectively), and more artists began to explore the medium's possibilities.[9] Clinton Adams authored a highly detailed history of these developments both inside and outside New York, noting that artists in Los Angeles began to work with lithography in the 1920s, when Mexican artist Jean Charlot arrived in the city and met printer Lynton Kistler.[10] Another center for lithographic printing emerged in Colorado Springs, where artist Boardman "Mike" Robinson began teaching in 1930. He invited New York lithographer Charles Locke to come for a summer, and Locke then trained Lawrence Barrett, who worked with artists visiting Robinson's school during the 1930s.[11] Grant Arnold pioneered lithographic printmaking in Woodstock, New York, over several summers while working as staff printer at the New York Art Students League during the rest of the year, and Emil Ganso also printed lithographs in Woodstock for himself and artist friends.[12]

Yet despite these opportunities—due to collectors' continuing preference for etchings and the additional cost of paying for a professional printer's assistance—intaglio techniques tended to predominate in art exhibitions. This did not change substantially until the mid-1930s, when the WPA-FAP Graphic Arts Division workshops made lithography an accessible, less costly option for artists who wished to experiment with its possibilities.

James Watrous's excellent, highly detailed history of American printmaking discusses numerous artists who became skilled printmakers during these decades, working with woodblock, wood engraving, and linocuts; the various intaglio media; lithography; and, later, silkscreen prints (serigraphy). His narrative features artists from this exhibition whose major focus was printmaking—such as Emilio Amero, Adolf Dehn, Fritz Eichenberg, Hugo Gellert, Martin Lewis, Margaret Lowengrund, Elizabeth Olds, and Charles Turzak—as well as those who

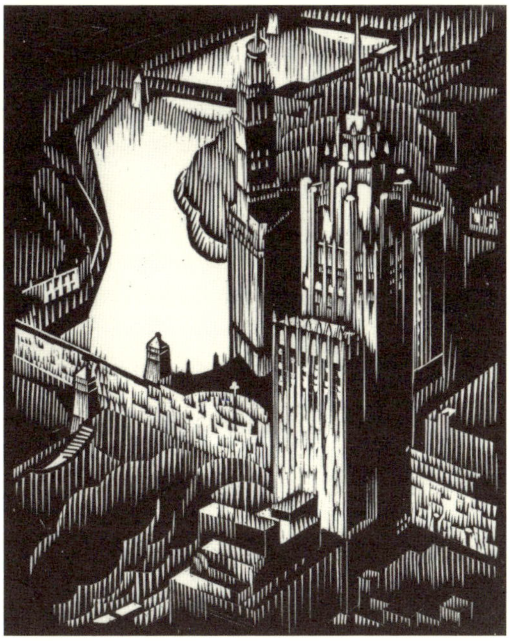

Fig. 1
Charles Turzak
American, 1899–1985
Chicago River, 1930
Woodcut
Cat. no. 51

developed expertise in both painting and printmaking, including Will Barnet, Harry Gottlieb, Rockwell Kent, Yasuo Kuniyoshi, Millard Sheets, Benton Spruance, and Harry Sternberg. The diverse works produced in all these media during the 1920s and early 1930s demonstrate that numerous artists across the country were actively engaged with printmaking well before the WPA-FAP workshops opened in 1935–36, and many of them continued to make prints independently during the late 1930s and into the following decade. One such example is Charles Turzak's 1930 woodcut *Chicago River* (fig. 1), one of a series he created portraying Chicago architectural landmarks. Another is Martin Lewis's *Passing Freight* (1938) (fig. 2), one of the highly subtle, technically nuanced nocturnal drypoints and etchings for which he was highly admired.

Yet the market for prints with modern American subjects was relatively slow to develop in the early twentieth century, and efforts to promote sales beyond single works displayed in gallery exhibitions had variable results. In 1912 John Sloan tried twice to sell a portfolio of ten urban etchings entitled *New York City Life* but met with very little success.[13] Perhaps the working-class subjects of his images were scorned by art collectors interested in creating an elegant domestic display with their works. A decade later, in 1924, when the *New Republic* advertised a portfolio of six original prints by several well-known artists, along with a subscription to the journal, for nine dollars, the response was more positive. By January 1925, the magazine announced that only a few sets remained, although no archival evidence of how many were included in the original offering exists.

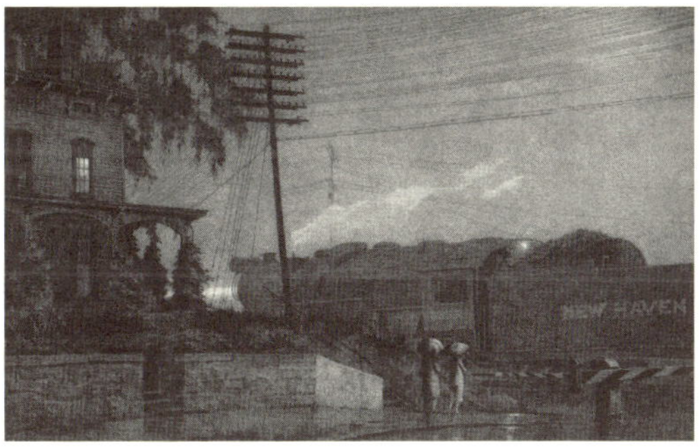

Fig. 2
Martin Lewis
American, 1881–1962
Passing Freight, 1938
Drypoint on ivory wove paper
Cat. no. 33

In the following decade, success in promoting print portfolios continued to be uncertain. In 1933 Hugo Gellert, an artist known for his radical leftist political stance, produced a portfolio of sixty lithographs entitled *Karl Marx's Capital in Lithographs*. After the successful sale of an edition printed in France, Gellert printed a second edition in New York in 1934, and then reproduced the same images in an inexpensive book. The lithographic crayon drawing style of Gellert's 1936 political print *Father Coughlin and His Flock* (fig. 3), showing the anti-Semitic "Radio Priest" at a microphone, is typical of his earlier work. The success of Gellert's prints suggests that, by the early 1930s, the Depression had rendered themes that critiqued capitalism acceptable to at least some American viewers, and by 1936 leftists were angry about the fascist violence implied in Coughlin's demagogic rhetoric.[14]

At the same time, ten artists working in New York formed the Contemporary Print Group with the intent to publish a series of portfolios that would each include six lithographs for fifteen dollars. The artists included newly famous Regionalists Thomas Hart Benton and John Steuart Curry, as well as Reginald Marsh and José Clemente Orozco. Most were already recognized as painters, but they hoped that this venture might provide some financial support during the early years of the Depression. They published two portfolios, but the subjects portrayed by several contributors—including sweatshop workers, strikers, and a lynching—proved to be too extreme for elite and

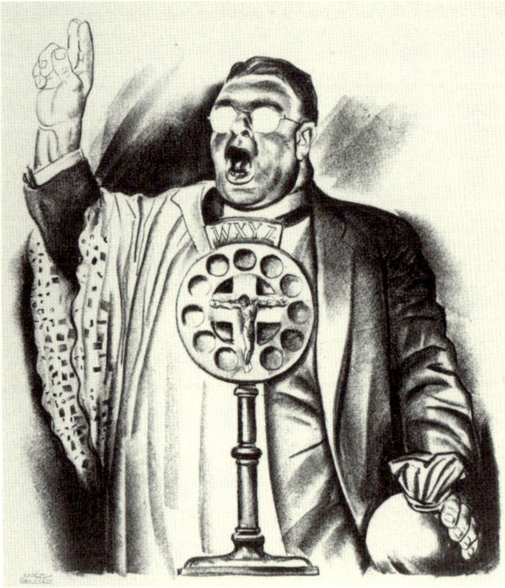

Fig. 3
Hugo Gellert
American, 1892–1985
Father Coughlin and His Flock, 1936
Lithograph on ivory wove paper
Cat. no. 22

middle-class collectors; neither portfolio sold well, and the group disbanded in 1934.[15]

The weight of the Depression's economic stresses also led Adolf Dehn to set up a print club in 1933 to promote his work; he sent out a brochure with illustrations of four prints, and for a fee of five dollars, subscribers could select one print to be delivered by mail.[16] Dehn later reported that this strategy was moderately successful. His 1940 color silkscreen *The Great God Pan* (fig. 4), with its mildly salacious depiction of a group of nuns painting in a springtime park while a naked god dances in a lake, is similar in style to his earlier witty—and, at times, sarcastic—lithographs, which were popular with educated viewers.

The idea of selling prints by mail to a new audience of middle-class art collectors was adopted to more commercial ends by Reeves Lewenthal, an entrepreneur who founded Associated American Artists in 1934. Despite its name, this was a sophisticated business enterprise: Lewenthal commissioned artists to produce etchings and lithographic prints, intending at first to sell them for five dollars each through national department store chains. When he discovered that some stores were reducing the prices of less popular works, he canceled their contracts, took out an ad in the *New York Times*, and quickly received $9,000 in orders. Lewenthal paid participating artists a flat $200 fee and distributed the signed prints in editions of 200 to 250 impressions. By 1935 an ad on the back cover of *Art Digest* offered subscribers a choice of works from a list of forty participating artists; Lewenthal also advertised in *Time* and *Reader's Digest*.

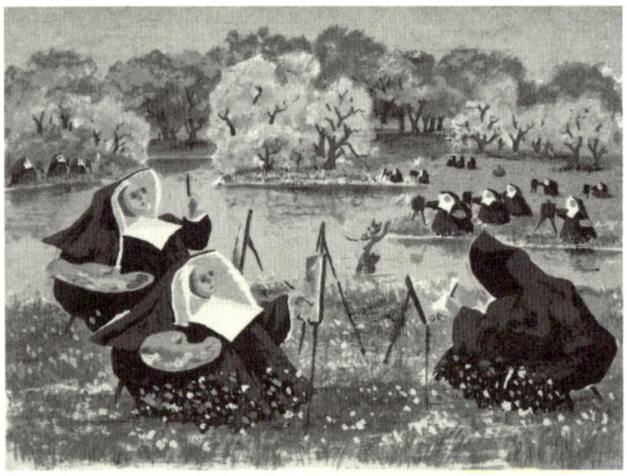

Fig. 4
Adolf Arthur Dehn
American, 1895–1968
The Great God Pan, 1940
Screenprint on cream wove paper
Cat. no. 15

Irwin Hoffman was one of the artists whom Lewenthal listed. His 1940 print *Taking a Fiver* (fig. 5), in the Needles collection, shows two industrial miners taking a quick cigarette break. Hoffman's two brothers were mining engineers, so he had first-hand experience of the tough working conditions and specific equipment associated with mining labor. Another work in the Needles collection, Joseph Hirsh's unsettling lithograph *The Hecklers* (1943) (fig. 6), was also commissioned by Associated American Artists. This print most likely addressed some contemporary social issue that has now faded into history. Lewenthal's prints-by-mail business continued to be successful into the mid-1940s, when changing tastes in art led the company to shift its focus from fine art to "artistic" household goods and furnishings.

Two other efforts to promote printmaking to a new mass audience in the mid-1930s are worth noting. The American Artists School, a renamed version of the earlier Communist-affiliated John Reed Club School of Art in New York, offered two print portfolios to subscribers in 1936 to raise funds for its programs. Each portfolio included five works with subjects that emphasized contemporary social justice themes from a leftist perspective; both portfolios included works by WPA-FAP artists and were printed in an edition of one hundred impressions. There is no record of how many portfolios sold, but the fact that a second portfolio was developed suggests that the first was reasonably successful. Growing support for leftist political views—connected to the Popular

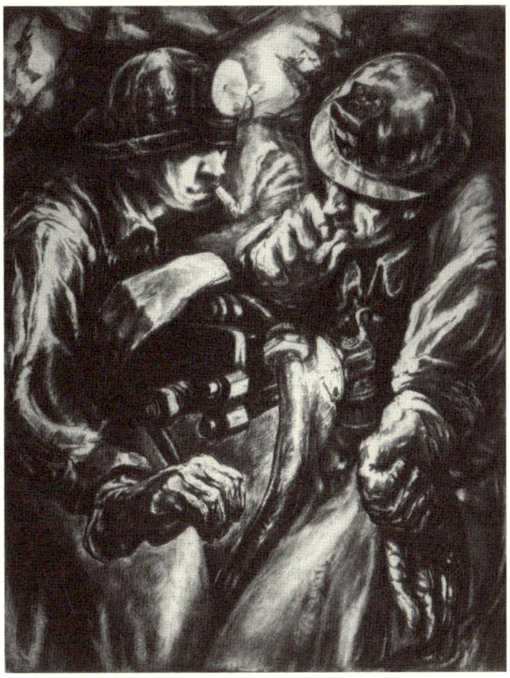

Fig. 5
Irwin Hoffman
American, 1901–1989
***Taking a Fiver,* 1940**
Etching
Collection of the DePaul Art Museum, Gift of Belverd Needles Jr. and Marian Powers Needles

Front against War and Fascism, a coalition of organizations ranging from the Communist Party to liberal anti-war groups—made prints with such themes more successful than they had been just a few years earlier.[17]

Another innovative project to bring public attention to prints drew on the WPA-FAP Graphic Arts Division's first year of production, but it was not limited to federally employed artists. In December 1936, printmakers associated with the American Artists' Congress against War and Fascism, founded in New York in 1935, organized the exhibition *America Today: One Hundred Prints*. Participating artists were limited to one print each, but the exhibition's designers took advantage of intaglio and lithographic prints' capacity for multiple originals, opening thirty duplicate exhibitions in venues across the country. A book with full-page reproductions of each of the prints accompanied the show; it was intended to further spread interest in printmaking as a decisively egalitarian form of fine art.[18] Critic Elizabeth McCausland reviewed the exhibition, praising its diversity by noting that "social themes and abstractions jostle each other; the popular and immediately appealing lithograph consorts with the stern and austere wood engraving."[19]

Yet no single contemporary exhibition could embrace all of the complex themes and techniques that 1930s printmakers were exploring, which are evident in the present exhibition and catalogue. In their woodcuts and wood engravings, etchings and aquatints, lithographs in black and white and in color, and silkscreen prints, artists portrayed images of industrial labor sites and workers' families, landscapes both rural and urban, scenes of unemployment and labor unrest (often with disingenuous titles such as Fritz Eichenberg's *April Showers* [fig. 7], which shows two burly policemen and a dejected, probably unemployed worker), and various other themes, including family groups, individual portraits, and a few abstractions. As Elizabeth Olds commented in a 1935 interview:

> American artists have lately chosen to portray our own life. We find our subjects on the streets, in the factory, the machines and workers of industry and on the farm. We aim to picture truly the life about us as the people we are in reference to the forces that make us. We choose all sides of life, searching for the vital and significant.[20]

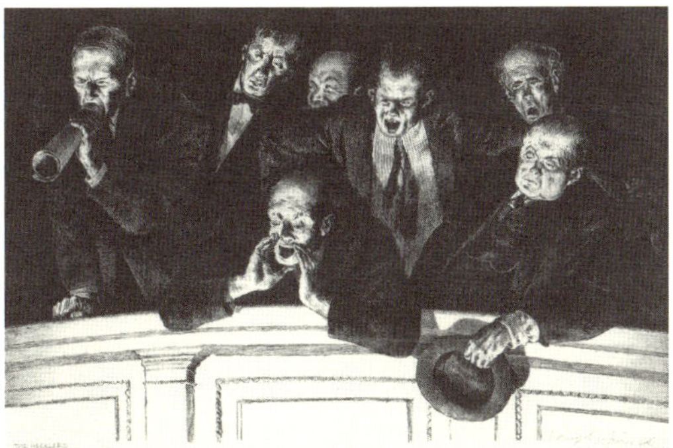

Fig. 6
Joseph Hirsch
American, 1910–1981
***The Hecklers,* 1943**
Lithograph on cream wove paper
Cat. no. 26

Olds had just finished working on the 1934–35 Public Works of Art Project in Omaha and would soon be on her way to New York to become a lead (experienced) artist at the WPA-FAP Graphic Arts Division workshop. The diversity she described was not only becoming typical of American printmaking, but was also gaining recognition in critical reviews and art magazines. In 1936 the magazine *Print Collectors Quarterly* began to include lithographs and woodcuts as well as etchings and engravings in its reviews, and it introduced a new feature entitled "Prints of Today" that promoted American artists. Likewise, *Art Digest* and *New Masses*, along with other media sources, featured information about print exhibitions held all over the country.

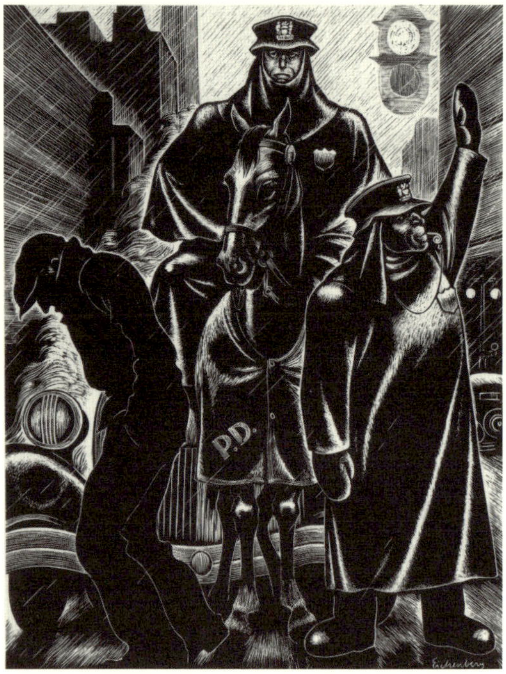

Fig. 7
Fritz Eichenberg
American, 1901–1990
***April Showers*, 1935**
Wood engraving
Cat. no. 18

The opening of the WPA-FAP Graphic Arts Division workshops—first in New York in December 1935 and then in six other cities—reflected this widening national interest in printmaking as a significant form of art production. There is an enormous quantity of literature on the Public Works of Art Project (PWAP) (1934–35) and the WPA-FAP (1925–43): Elizabeth Seaton's excellent dissertation "Federal Prints and Democratic Culture," for example, is filled with valuable information gleaned from intensive study of archival sources and thoughtful analyses of how contemporary discussions of democratic ideals were played out in the rhetoric of WPA administrators. Seaton noted that, at its height, the entire FAP employed 790 artists in 36 cities, but most printmaking activities were centered in seven major cities with established Graphic Arts Division workshops: Boston, Chicago, Cleveland, Los Angeles, New York, Philadelphia, and San Francisco. Groups of printmakers also worked together under FAP auspices in Albuquerque, Denver, Des Moines, Detroit, Madison, Milwaukee, Minneapolis, Monterey, New Orleans, Oakland, Portland (OR), Providence (RI), Santa Barbara, Seattle, Woodstock (NY), and other smaller communities.[21] Over 239,000 different images were editioned by FAP artists.[22] The artists received three proofs from each edition, which would typically have included twenty-five impressions. The rest, which were intended to be disbursed to various governmental and public institutions, were supposed to be marked with a WPA stamp, although this rule was not always carefully enforced. Because they were generally small, many of these works quietly disappeared from their originally assigned sites after the FAP closed down in 1943. Today the fact that a print lacks a WPA stamp does not necessarily illuminate whether it was made as part of the FAP.[23]

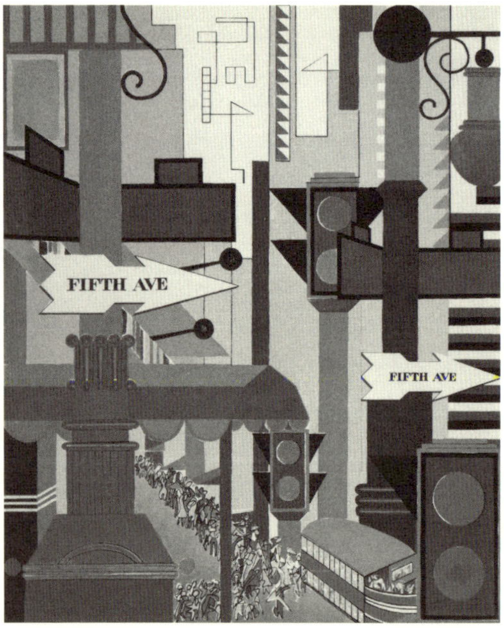

Fig. 8
Mildred Rackley
American, 1906–1992
***Fifth Avenue*, 1939–1940**
Screenprint
Cat. no. 40

In 1972 art historian Francis V. O'Connor published *The New Deal Art Projects: An Anthology of Memoirs*, which includes an essay by Jacob Kainen about the Graphic Arts Division.[24] Kainen explained the establishment and procedures of the New York workshop in detail and outlined its beneficial aspects as well as the restrictions that frustrated many participants. Overall, most artists employed by the WPA-FAP believed that they benefited from federal support for the arts. The Graphic Arts Division workshops provided artists with an almost utopian environment of artistic camaraderie and educational opportunities. They brought together an enlivening mix of experienced artists and ambitious individuals just out of art school, and women were hired on an almost equal basis with their male peers.[25] Workshop administrators were generally highly supportive of technical experiments, particularly the development of color lithography and silkscreen printmaking (renamed serigraphy to give it a more serious status), although somewhat less enthusiastic about abstract stylistic innovation. Mildred Rackley's modernist silkscreen print *Fifth Avenue* (fig. 8), created in 1939–40, with its stylized geometric syncopation, offers a lively example of artists' interests in using the new medium of silkscreen along with jazzy stylistic ideas to develop color images that would attract middle-class art buyers.

Despite these positive qualities of the WPA-FAP, problems with federal support for artists certainly existed.[26] Although frustrating time-keeping requirements—artists had to sign in daily at a central office, although they were allowed to work in their own studios—were eventually dropped, the instigation of a limit on employment to eighteen months, set by a federal mandate in 1939, forced artists in continuing financial need to resign and risk the vagaries of the reapplication process. Other restrictions, such as a loyalty oath (first required in 1940), led some artists employed by the WPA-FAP to leave the workshops, even as hostile members of Congress repeatedly threatened to completely cut funding.[27] Moreover, many artists, especially those with militant political views, felt that they were under constant pressure to defend the value of government sponsorship of art production and ideals of cultural democracy. Finally, the government was also less than effective in finding ways to employ non-white artists. By 1940, with the FAP already facing debilitating cuts in funding, it became clear that, despite intense efforts to persuade Congress to establish a permanent Federal Art Bureau, this goal would never be realized.[28] The social values of egalitarian idealism and cultural diversity that underwrote the FAP's founding collapsed under the pressures of the slow economic recovery at the end of the decade, anti-Communist red-baiting, and finally the onset of World War II.

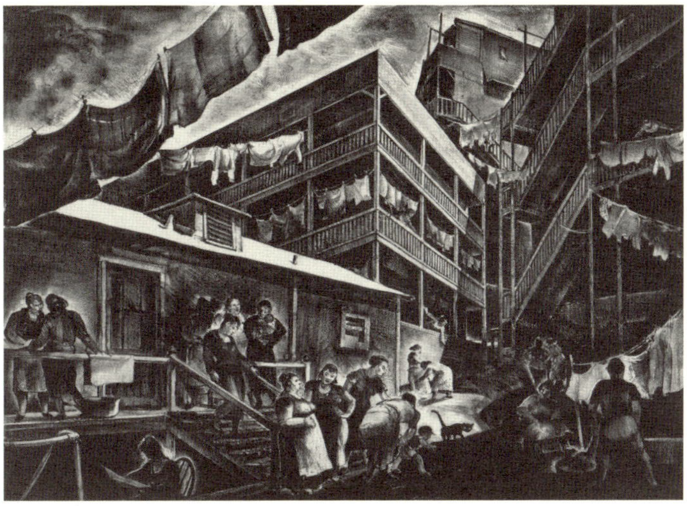

Fig. 9
Millard Owen Sheets
American, 1907–1989
***Family Flats*, 1935**
Lithograph on cream wove paper
Cat. no. 44

Nevertheless, throughout the 1930s, the value of cultural democracy for the arts was a concept prevalent in much New Deal rhetoric—articulated by Holger Cahill, director of the FAP, and echoed in the speeches and writing of numerous other WPA-FAP administrators and program directors.[29] They all strongly encouraged the belief that works of art could support national democratic values by educating, enlivening, and unifying the country's diverse communities.[30] Indeed, the importance of cultural democracy and the value of cultural diversity were both affirmed in 1930s discourse—in relation to national and regional identities, forms of artistic production, and the validation of differing aesthetic preferences.

It was these ideals of cultural democracy that legitimated the widely varied subject choices and visual strategies that characterize the works in this exhibition. Two examples created on opposite sides of the country illustrate these qualities: Millard Sheets's 1935 lithograph *Family Flats* (fig. 9), produced in Los Angeles; and Benton Spruance's 1936 lithograph *The People Work: Morning* (fig. 10), created in Philadelphia. While both works feature crowds of people and angular architectural settings, each artist devised a highly individualized depiction specific to his own

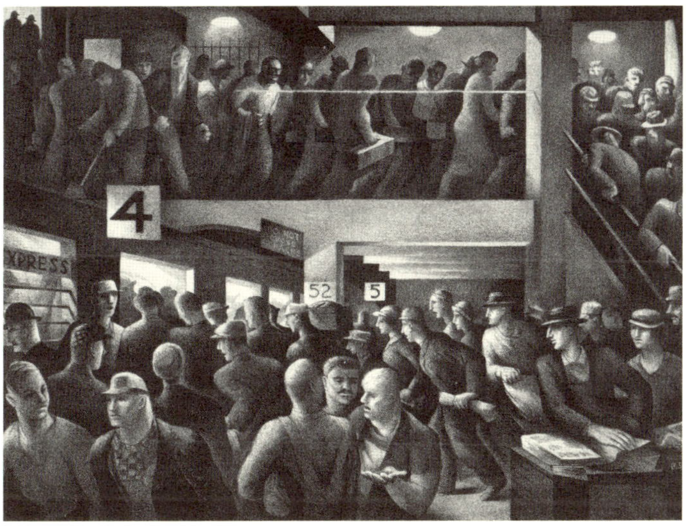

Fig 10
Benton Spruance
American, 1904–1967
***The People Work: Morning*, 1936**
Lithograph on cream wove paper
Cat. no. 46

experience: for Spruance, dense crowds of urban workers surging onto a subway platform; for Sheets, the very different drama of working-class wash lines and social interactions in a more leisurely West Coast setting.

In the context of cultural democracy, FAP administrators encouraged artists to view themselves from a newly positive perspective—no longer as distanced aesthetes, belligerent social critics, or unreliable bohemians, but instead as useful workers, able to connect the private sphere of cultural production with government efforts to promote aesthetic literacy, community uplift, and the reconstruction of a democratic national identity.[31] Their works were also promoted to the public as vital to daily life and cultural improvement. Edward Bruce, director of the Public Works of Art Project and later the Treasury Section of Fine Arts, suggested that federal art programs could take the "snobbery out of art and make it the daily food of the average citizen."[32] Cahill said that his goal as director of the FAP was not to facilitate the production of a few outstanding masterpieces, but to make art "a vital, functioning part of any cultural scheme."[33] Lewis Mumford, a cultural critic not directly associated with the government projects, similarly commented in 1936 that the WPA-FAP had given artists "something more precious than their daily bread: they have at last achieved the liberty to perform an essential function in life, in the knowledge that their work has a destination in the community."[34] Speaking specifically about prints, Gustave von Groschwitz, the supervisor of the New York Graphic Arts Division workshop, argued that "the dramatic value of the print, its moderate size and the fact that it can be held in the hand" all demonstrated the democratic accessibility of printmaking as a significant form of American artistic production.[35]

In his introduction to the catalogue for the exhibition *American Art Today* at the 1939 World's Fair, Cahill summed up these perspectives: "Probably there has never before been a period in our country's history when the graphic arts could show such a high level of quality, such versatility, such technical competence in a broad range of media."[36] This was true across the country—and not only in relation to the FAP. As scholar James Watrous observed, "Despite discouragements which all the arts endured in the years of the Great Depression, accomplished printmaking was done whether or not the individual artists were the beneficiaries of federal support."[37] He added that the works produced in the 1930s and early 1940s were "an odd lot of fine and inferior prints which, regardless of their differing merits, confirmed a maturing of the art." Thus, it becomes evident that the "national school," evoked by Carl Zigrosser in his 1942 comments on the development of graphic arts in America, was characterized not by any single dominant style or exploration of any single medium, but by an expanding diversity of interests supported by a wide range of individuals, organizations, and institutions. That lively expansiveness is evident in this exhibition, expressed through the values of cultural democracy and diversity that so significantly shaped the New Deal era.

1. Two of the most comprehensive accounts of developments in American printmaking from 1900 through the 1940s are found in James Watrous, *A Century of American Printmaking, 1880–1980* (Madison: University of Wisconsin Press, 1984); and Clinton Adams, *American Lithographers, 1900–1960: The Artists and Their Printers* (Albuquerque: University of New Mexico Press, 1983).

2. Benton Spruance, "The Place of the Printmaker," *Magazine of Art* (Oct. 1937): 615–18.

3. Carl Zigrosser, *The Artist in America* (New York: Alfred A. Knopf, 1942), viii.

4. Walt Whitman, "Democratic Vistas," in *Complete Poetry and Selected Prose by Walt Whitman*, ed. James E. Miller (New York: Houghton Mifflin, 1959), 479. This was cited in relation to the views of cultural critic Lewis Mumford in A. Joan Saab, *For the Millions: American Art and Culture between the Wars* (Philadelphia: University of Pennsylvania Press, 2004).

5. See David Acton, "Printmaking Communities in Southern California, 1900–1960," in *Proof: The Rise of Printmaking in Southern California*, ed. Leah Lehmbeck (Los Angeles: Getty Publications/Norton Simon Museum, 2011), 55–57.

6. Elizabeth Gaede Seaton, "Federal Prints and Democratic Culture: The Graphic Arts Division of the Works Progress Administration Federal Art Project, 1935–1943," (PhD diss., Northwestern University, 2000), 6, 17.

7. See, for instance, Robert L. Crump, *Minnesota Prints and Printmakers, 1900–1945* (St. Paul: Minnesota Historical Society Press, 2009).

8. Watrous, *American Printmaking*, 81.

9. Adams, *American Lithographers*, 49–120.

10. Kistler shifted his expertise from commercial printing to fine-art lithography. Ibid., 100–08.

11. Ibid., 109–11.

12. Watrous, *American Printmaking*, 59–69.

13. Ibid., 44–46.

14. Helen Langa, *Radical Art: Printmaking and the Left in 1930s New York* (Berkeley: University of California Press, 2004), 15.

15. Ibid., 16–17.

16. Ibid., 15; Adams, *American Lithographers*, 139.

17. See Virginia Hagelstein Marquardt and Sylvan Cole, "American Artists School's Print Series of 1936," *Print Quarterly* 6, no. 4 (1989): 416–21; Langa, *Radical Art*, 21, 244, n. 39.

18. Ibid., 20–21.

19. Elizabeth McCausland, "American Today—A Graphic Art Experiment," *Prints* 7, no. 2 (Dec. 1936): 110–11.

20. Elizabeth Olds, interview with the *Omaha World-Tribune*, 1935; quoted in Susan E. Arthur, "Elizabeth Olds: Artist of the People and the Times," in Susan E. Arthur and Kenneth Prescott, *Elizabeth Olds, Retrospective Exhibition: Paintings, Drawings, Prints* (Austin, TX: RKG Foundation, 1986), 14.

21. Seaton, "Federal Prints," 6–7. Printmaking was also taught at WPA-FAP Community Art Centers, such as the Harlem Center in New York, the South Side Community Arts Center in Chicago, and the Walker Art Center in Minneapolis.

22. Seaton, "Federal Prints," iii.

23. For more information about WPA-FAP art works, see the General Services WPA Art Inventory and Recovery website (http://www.gsaig.gov/index.cfm/other-documents/other/works-progress-administration-wpa-art-recovery-project/ [accessed June 12, 2014]). There is as yet no digital master list of all WPA-FAP prints. The best print resource is *WPA Artwork in Non-Federal Repositories, Edition II* (Washington D.C.: U.S. General Services Administration, Fine Arts Program, December 1999).

24. Jacob Kainen, "The Graphic Arts Division of the WPA Federal Art Project," in *The New Deal Art Projects: An Anthology of Memoirs*, ed. Francis V. O'Connor (Washington, D.C.: Smithsonian Institution Press, 1972), 155–76.

25. For more discussion of these disparities, see Langa, *Radical Art*.

26. For some complications related to egalitarian ideals, see Helen Langa, "Egalitarian Vision, Gendered Experience: Women Printmakers and the WPA/FAP Graphic Arts Workshop," in *The Expanding Discourse: Feminism and Art History*, eds. Norma Broude and Mary D. Garrard (New York: HarperCollins, 1992): 408–23. See also Seaton, *Federal Prints*.

27. This eventually occurred in 1943. Kainen, "The Graphic Arts Division," 163; see also Langa, *Radical Art*, 204–24. For more on the tensions within WPA-FAP workshop culture, see Helen Langa, "Constructing Cultural Democracy: Ideology, Economics, and Public Art in 1930s America," in *The Political Economy of Art: Making the Nation of Culture*, ed. Julie F. Codell (Teaneck, NJ: Fairleigh Dickinson University Press/Rosemont Publishing & Printing Corp., 2008), 170–71.

28. Langa, *Radical Art*, 208–10; Langa, "Constructing Cultural Democracy," 175.

29. Seaton observed that the ideas and even specific phrasing used by Cahill in speeches, essays, and reports were borrowed and repeated by other arts administrators in exhibition catalogues and press releases, and even in articles penned by artists and critics, confirming (or at least leading to the appearance of) a widely shared affirmation of the value of cultural democracy. Seaton, "Federal Prints," 18.

30. Langa, "Constructing Cultural Democracy," 163.

31. Ibid.

32. Letter from Edward Bruce to Admiral Peoples (Nov. 14, 1934). Bruce MSS, Reel D89, Archives of American Art, Smithsonian Institution. Cited in Marlene Park and Gerald Markowitz, *Democratic Vistas: Post Offices and Public Art in the New Deal* (Philadelphia: Temple University Press, 1984), 8, n. 16.

33. Holger Cahill, *New Horizons in American Art* (New York: Museum of Modern Art, 1936), 18.

34. Lewis Mumford, "A Letter to the President," *New Republic* 89 (Dec. 30, 1936): 264.

35. Gustave von Groshwitz, "Prints for the People" (Jan. 1937); quoted in Seaton, "Federal Prints," 50.

36. Holger Cahill, "American Art Today," in *American Art Today* (Poughkeepsie, NY: Apollo Press, 1987), 32.

37. Watrous, *American Printmaking*, 122.

Catalogue of the Exhibition

All works are gifts to the collection of the DePaul Art Museum from Belverd Needles Jr. and Marian Powers Needles.

Dimensions of images are given in inches; height precedes width.

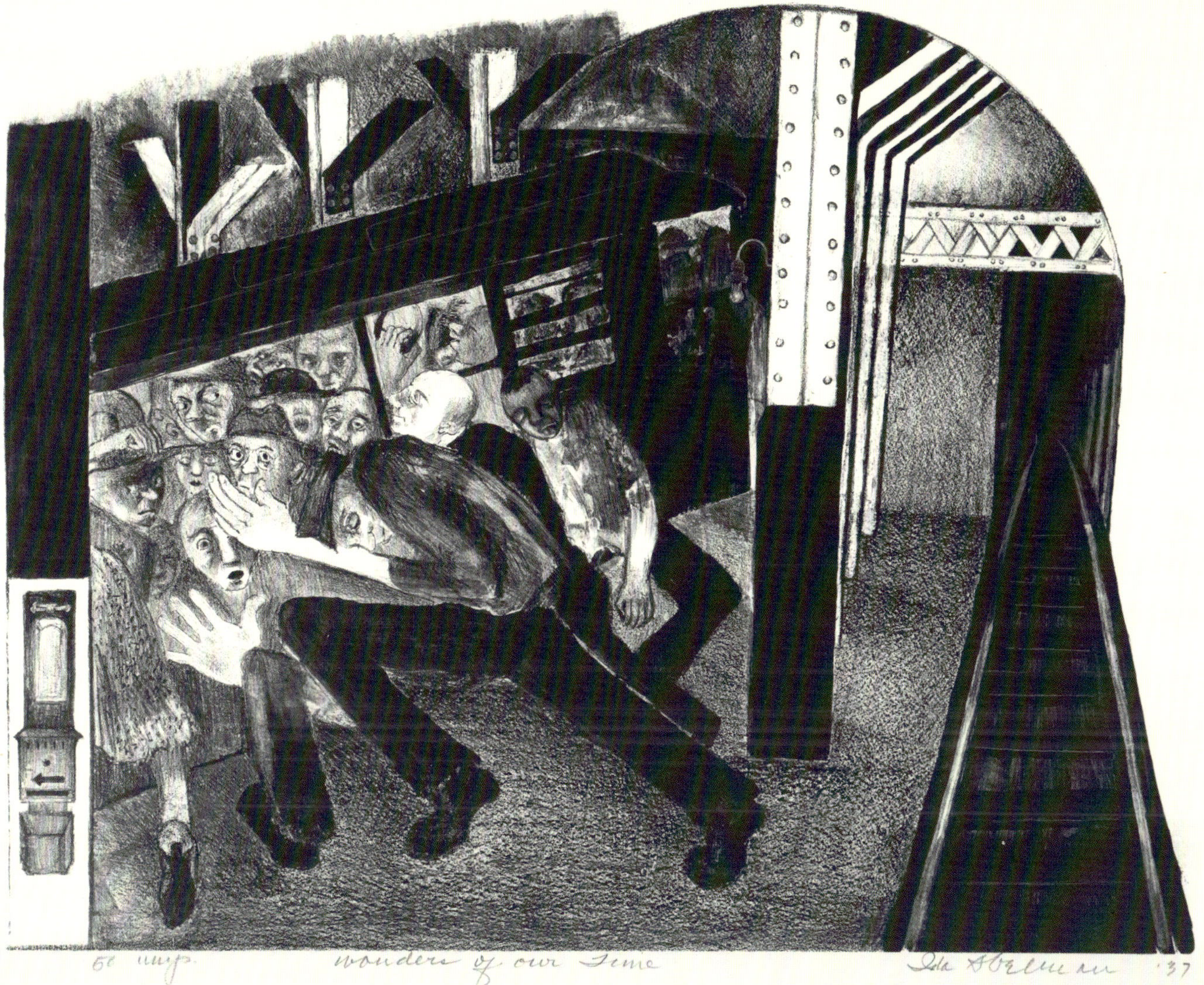

1
Ida Abelman
American, 1910–2002
Wonders of Our Time, 1937
Lithograph on ivory wove paper,
7 1⁄16 × 16 7⁄8

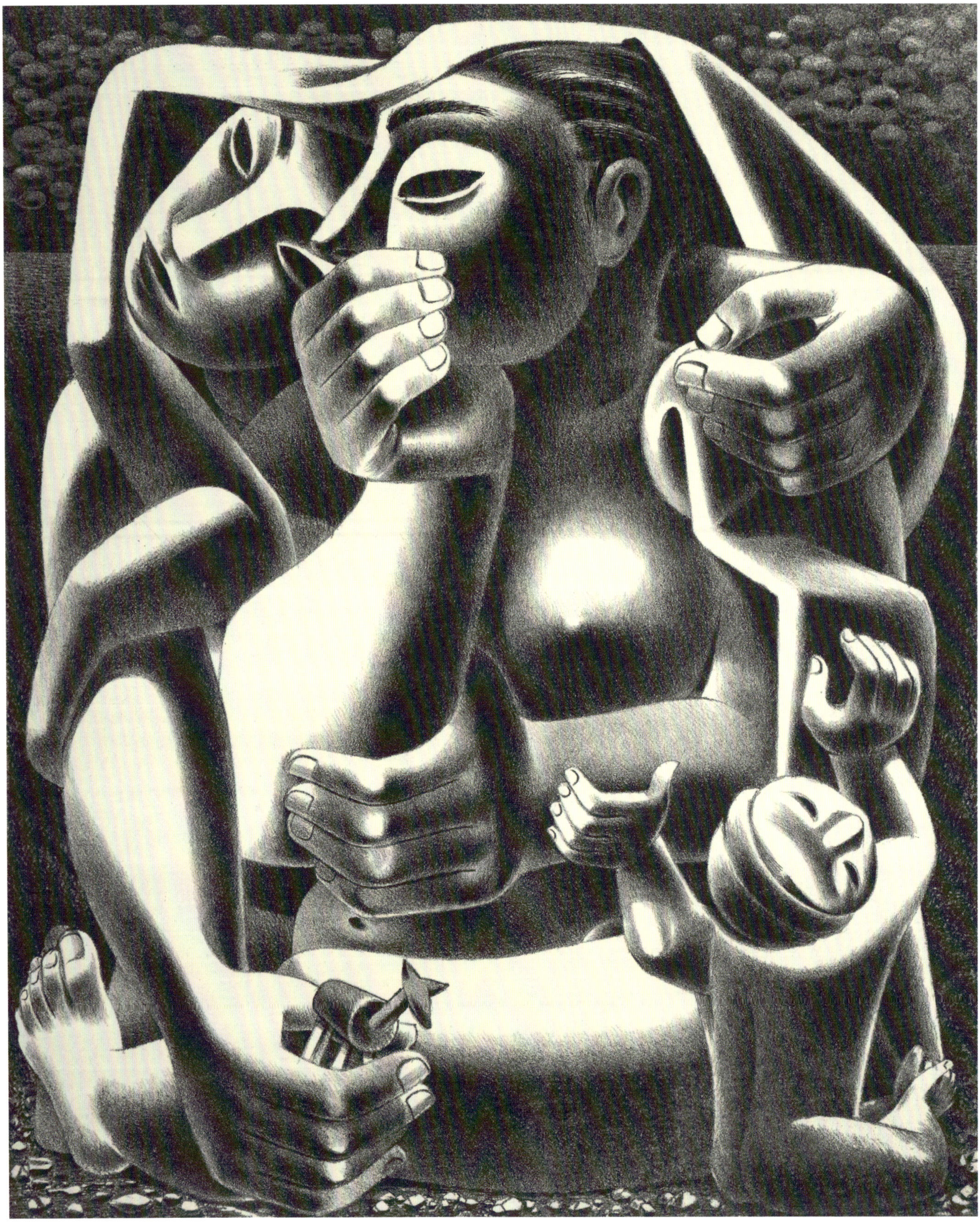

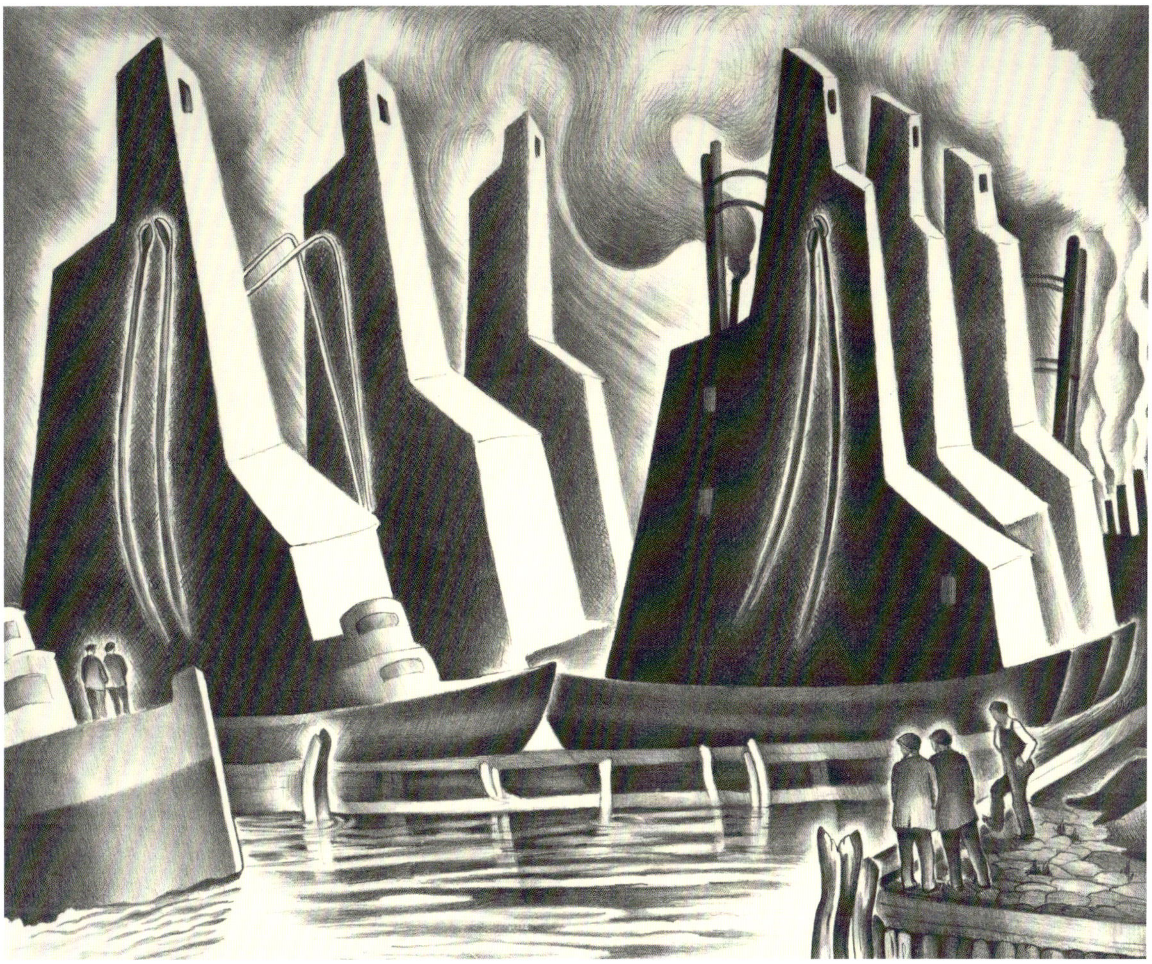

2
Emilio Amero
American, 1901–1976
Where, 1940
Lithograph on cream wove paper,
12 3/8 x 10 3/16

3
Vera Andrus
American 1896–1979
New Jersey Cyclops, 1940
Lithograph on white wove paper,
4 1/2 x 6 1/8

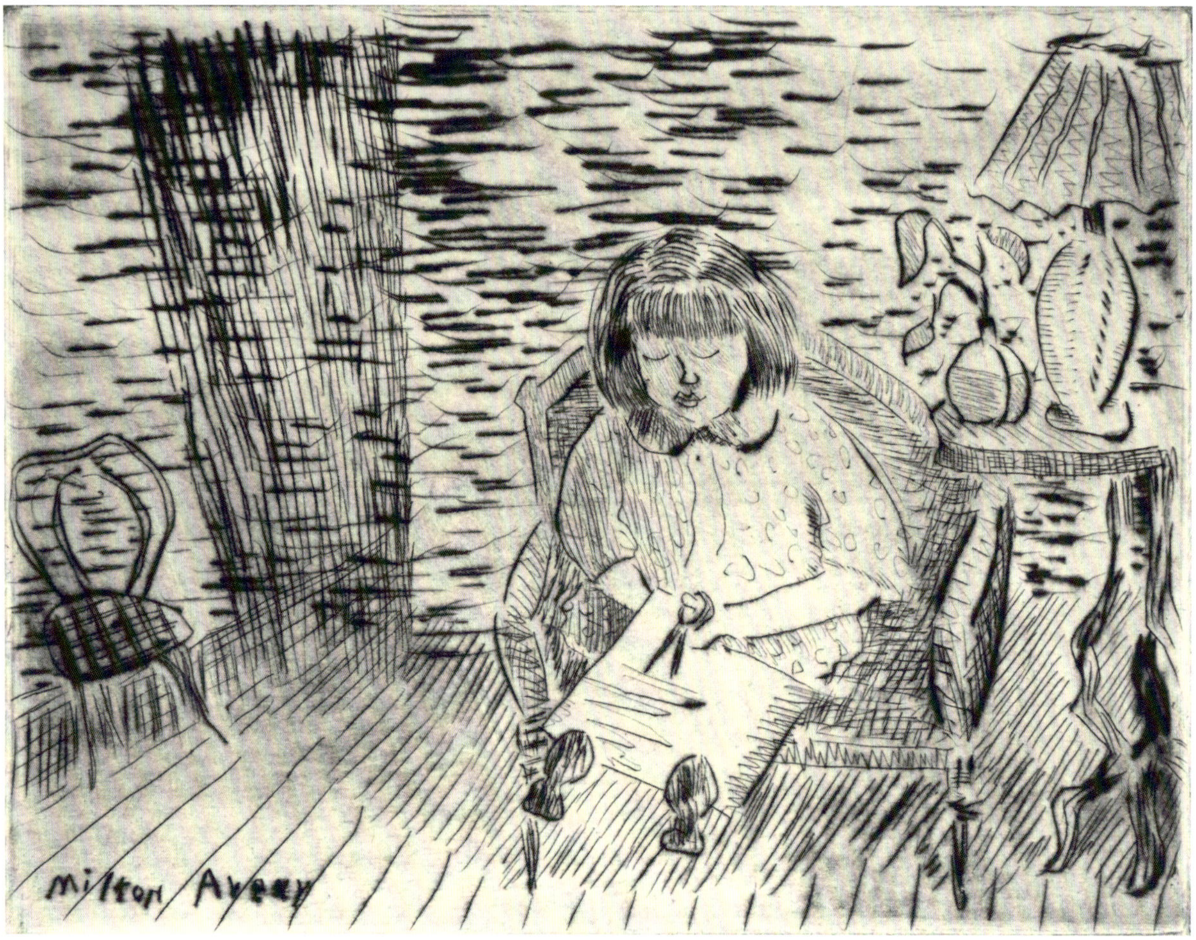

4
Milton Avery
American, 1885–1965
Child Cutting, 1936
Drypoint, 5 ¼ x 6 ¾

5
Will Barnet
American, 1911–2012
Sleeping Mother, 1940
Etching, 9 ⅞ x 10 ¾

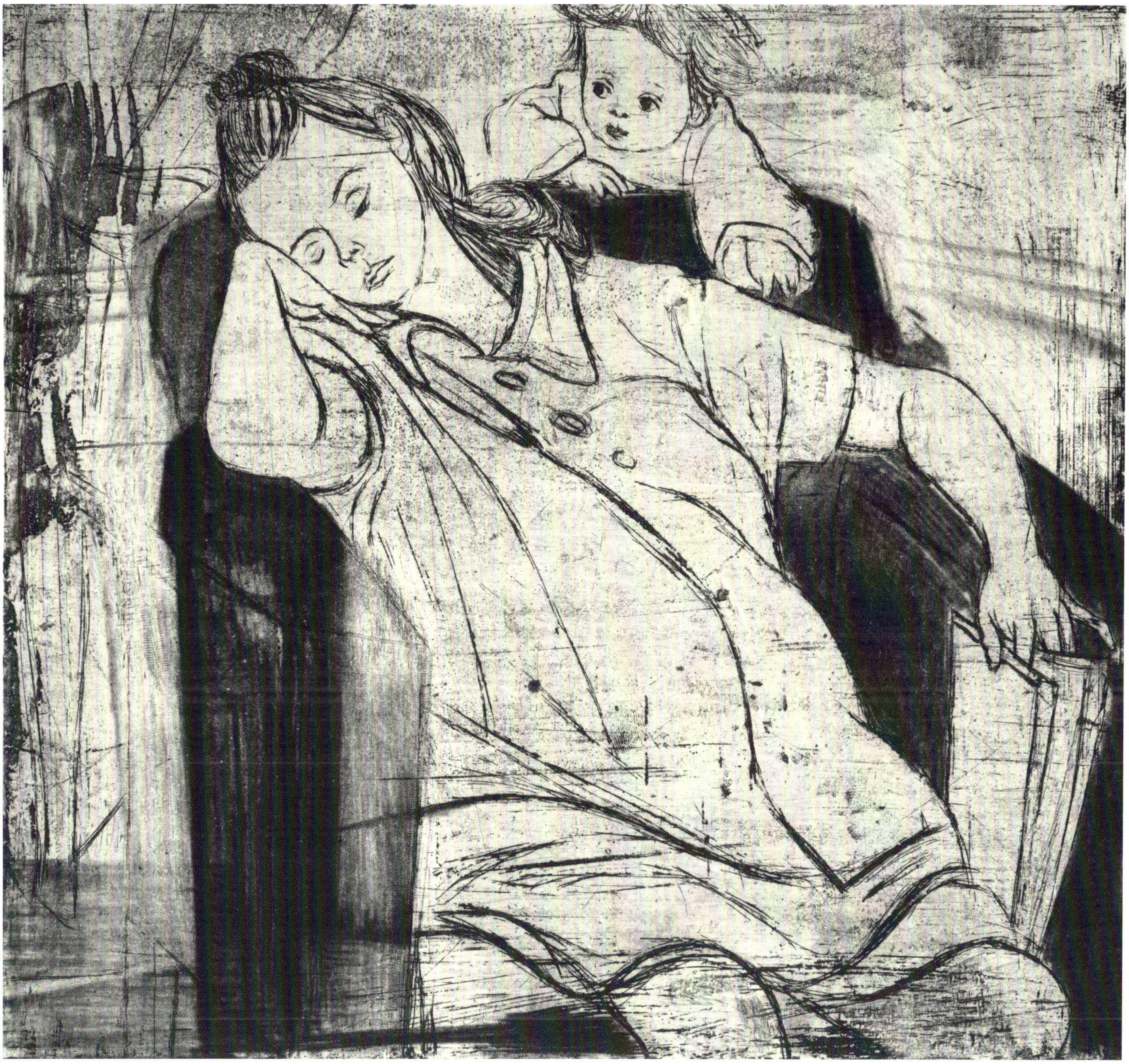

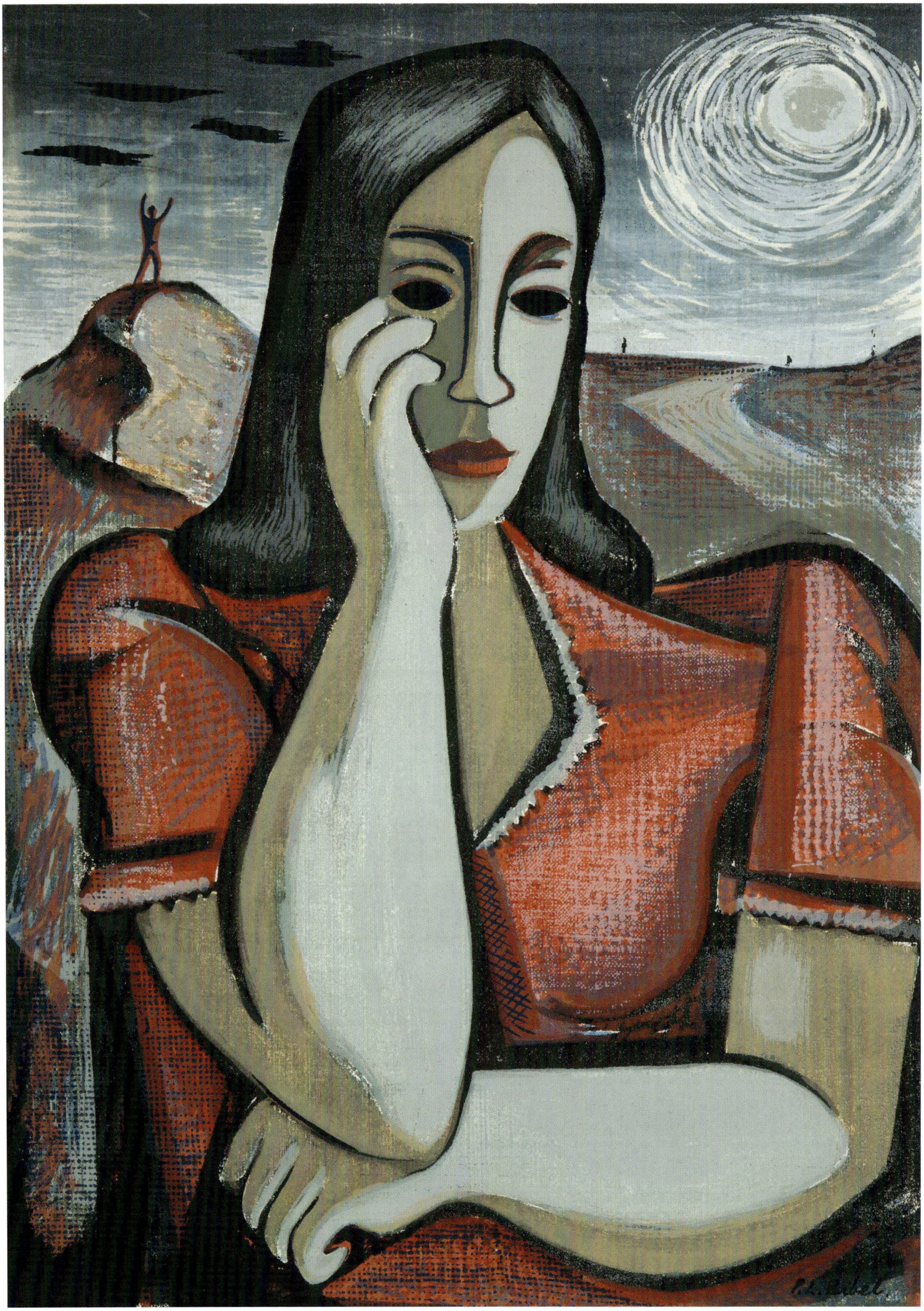

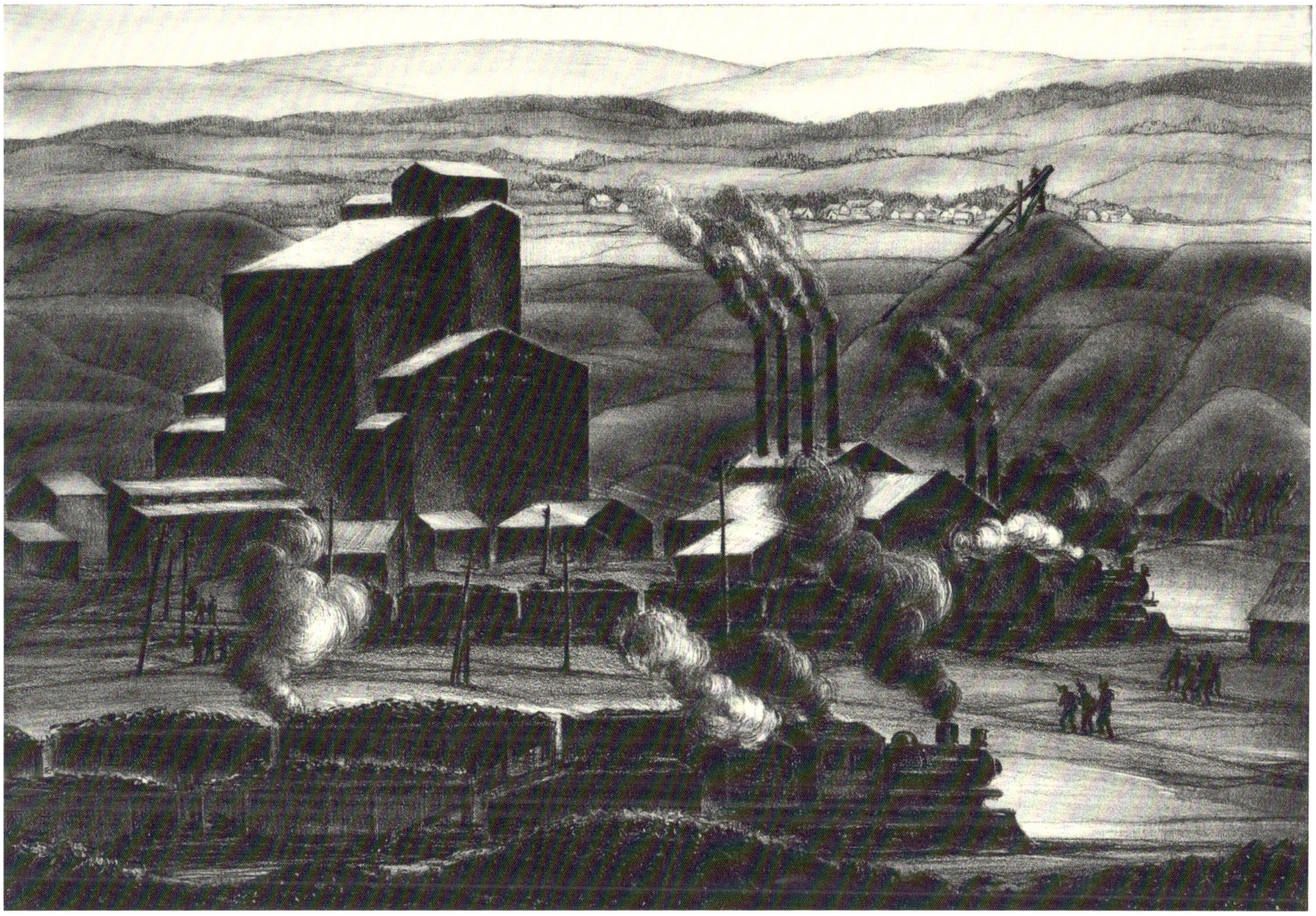

6
Leon Bibel
American, 1913–1995
Nocturne, 1938
Color screenprint, 19 × 13 ⅞

7
Esther Brock Bird
American, 1888–1950
Anthracite Mine, Carbondale, Pa. II, 1935
Lithograph on white wove paper, 8 ¾ × 13

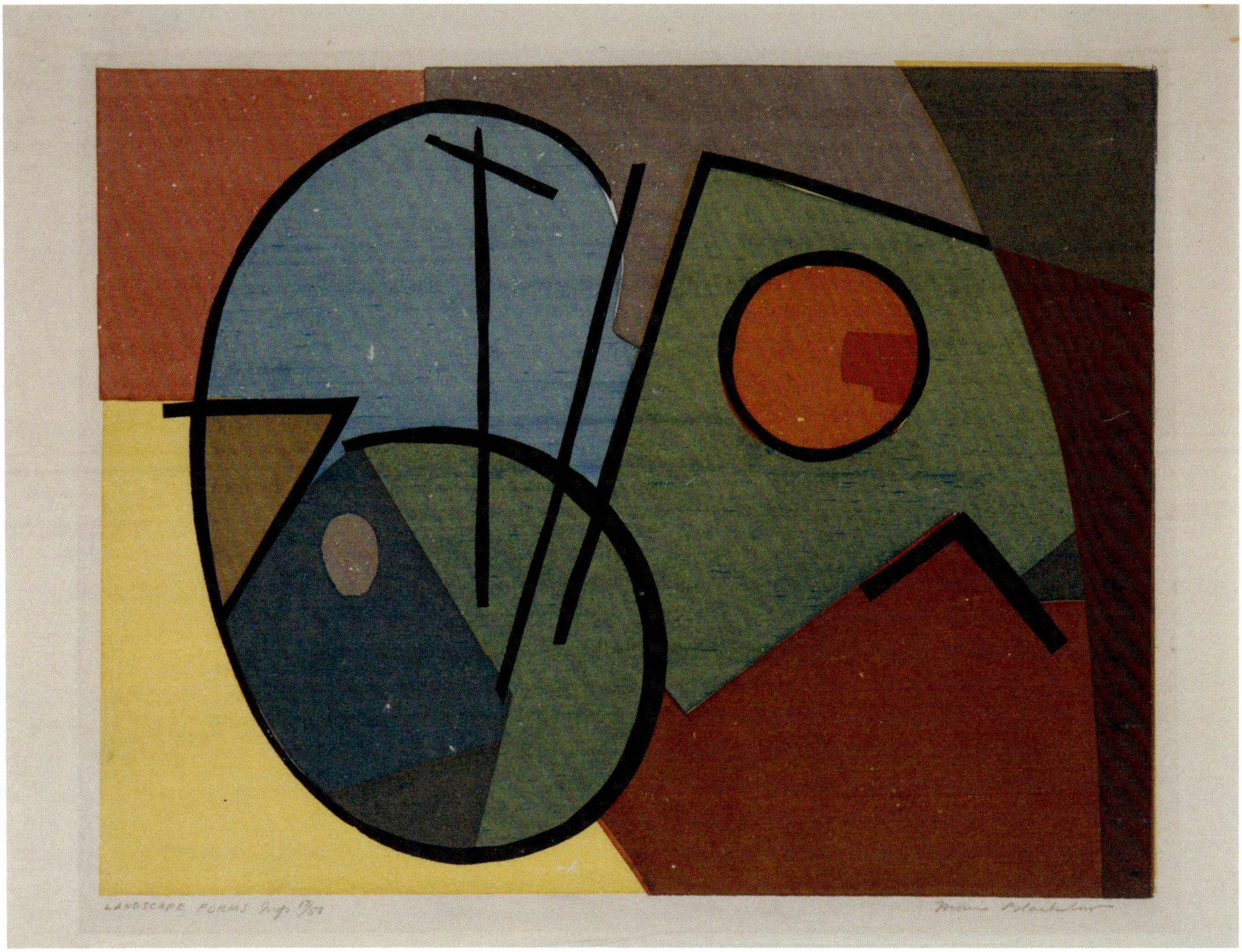

8

Morris Atkinson Blackburn

American, 1902–1979

Landscape Forms, 1944

Screenprint, 9 1/8 × 11 7/8

9

Abe Blashko

American, 1921–2011

The Pillars, 1939

Lithograph on white wove paper, 19 1/4 × 12 1/8

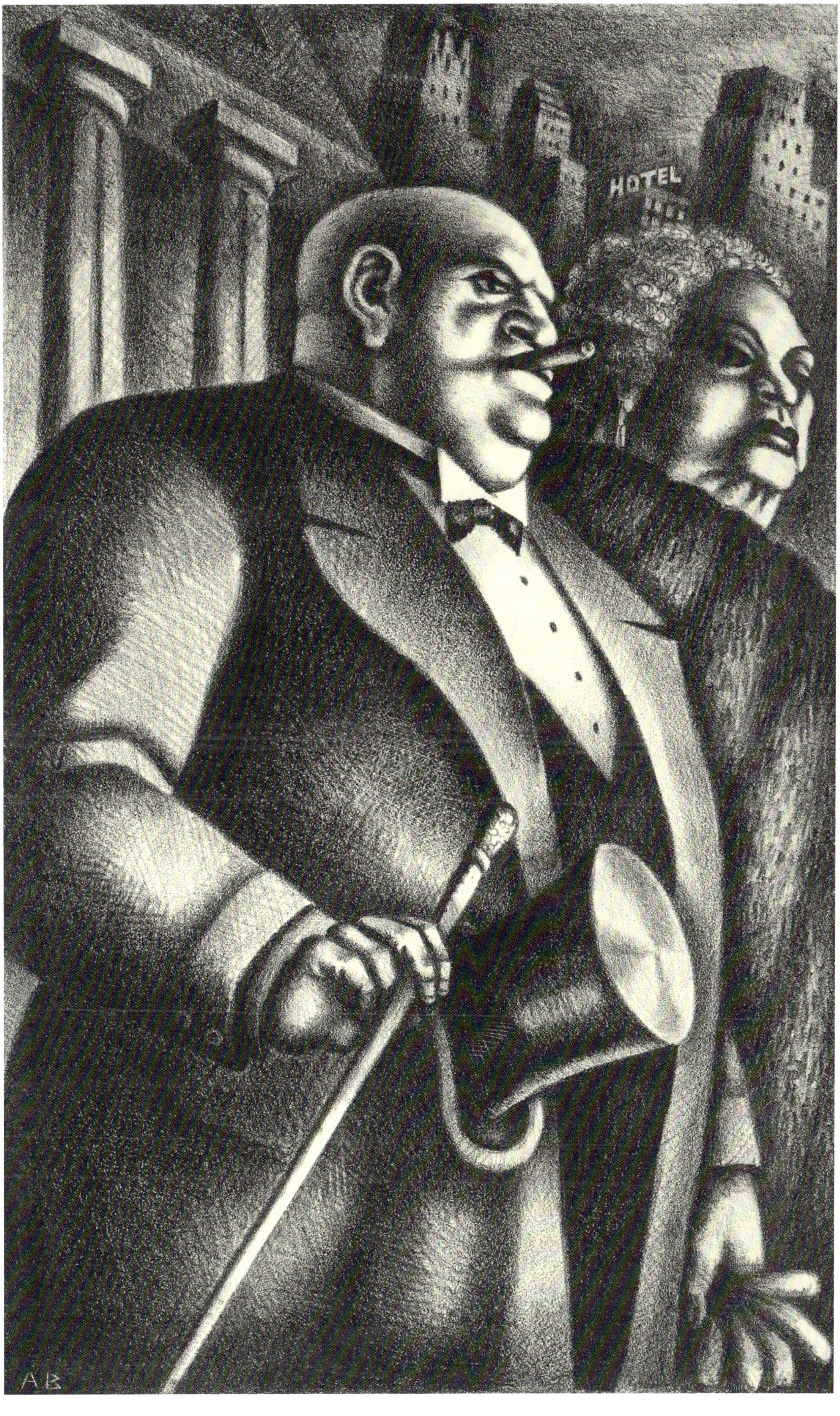
HOTEL
AB

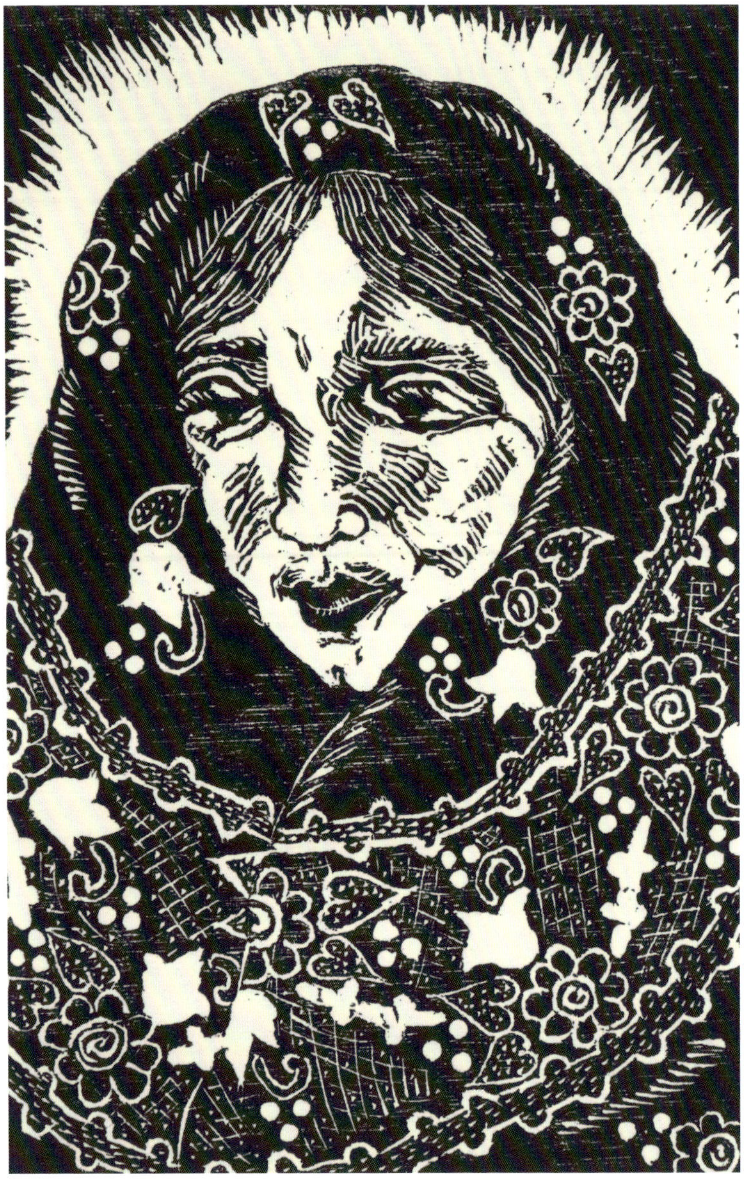

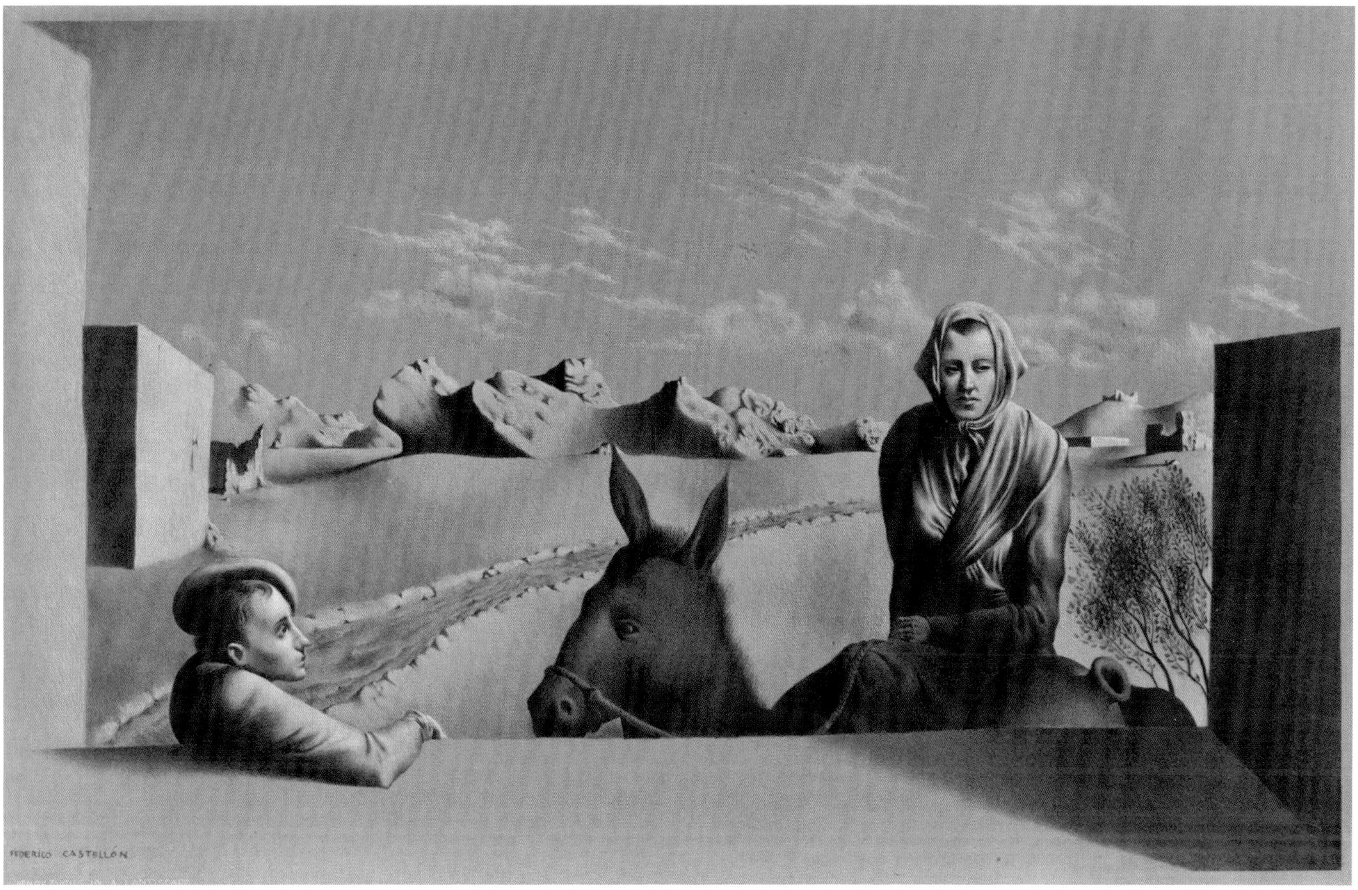

10
Fritzi Brod
American, 1900–1952
Peasant Woman, 1936
Woodcut on white wove paper, 6 x 3 ⅞

11
Federico Cristencia de Castellón y Martinez
American, born Spain 1914–1971
Rendezvous in a Landscape, 1939
Color lithograph on ivory wove paper, 9 ⅝ x 15 ⅛

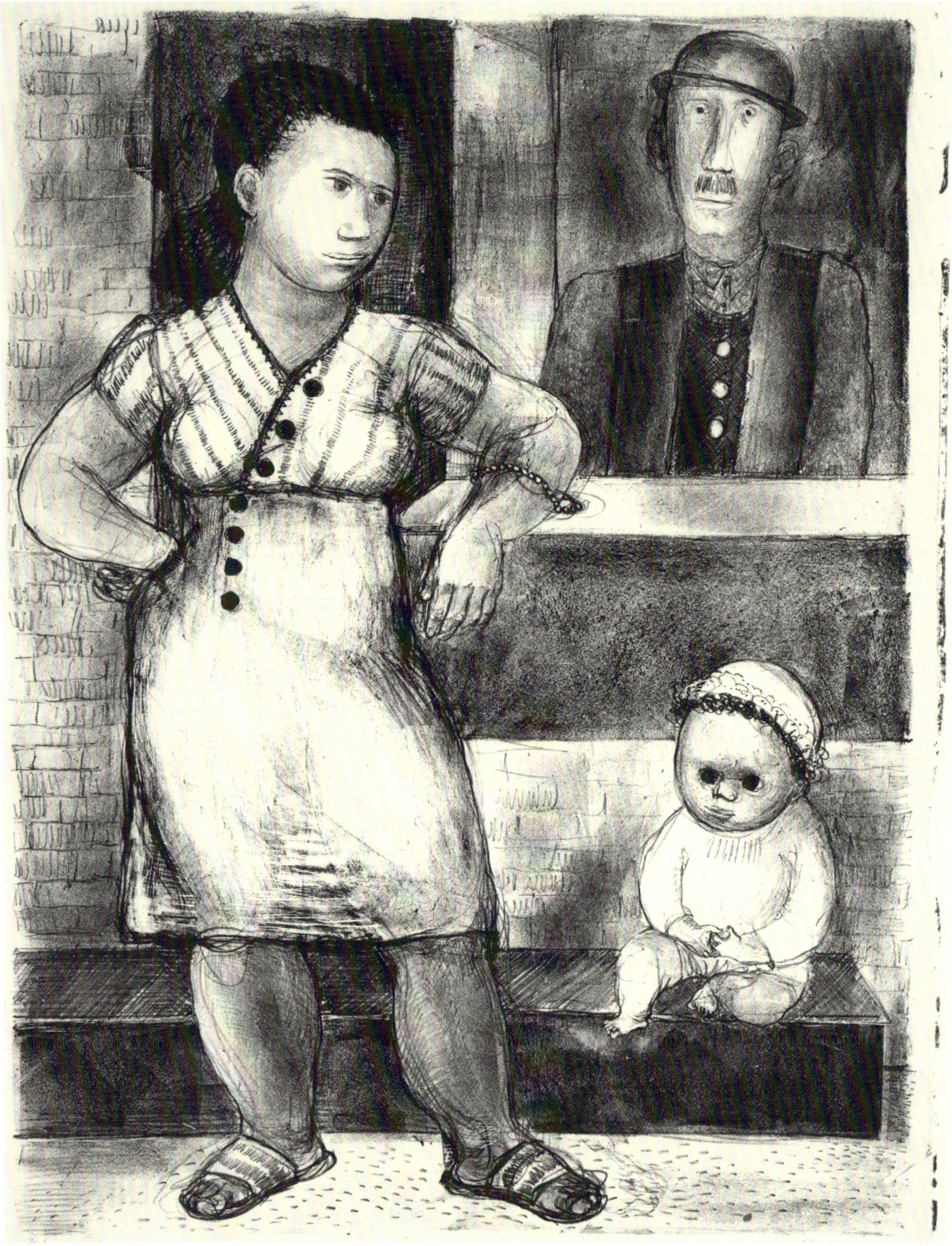

12
Eleanor Coen
American, 1916–2010
Untitled (Couple with baby), 1938
Lithograph on ivory wove paper, 12 ⅛ x 9 ¼

13
James Daugherty
American, 1889–1974
Victory, 1945
Linocut, 18 ⅞ x 12 ½

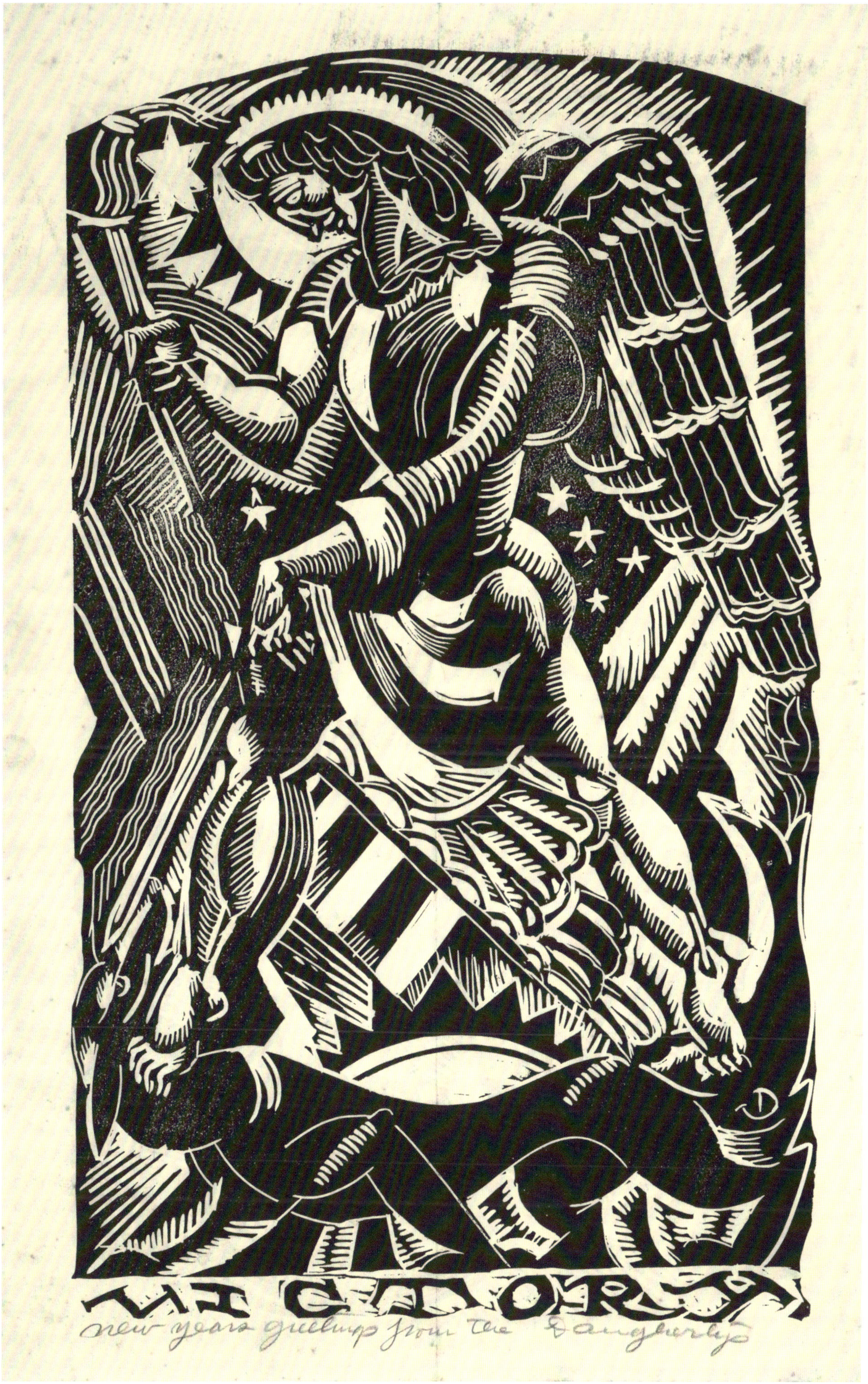
VICTORY
new years greetings from the Daughertys

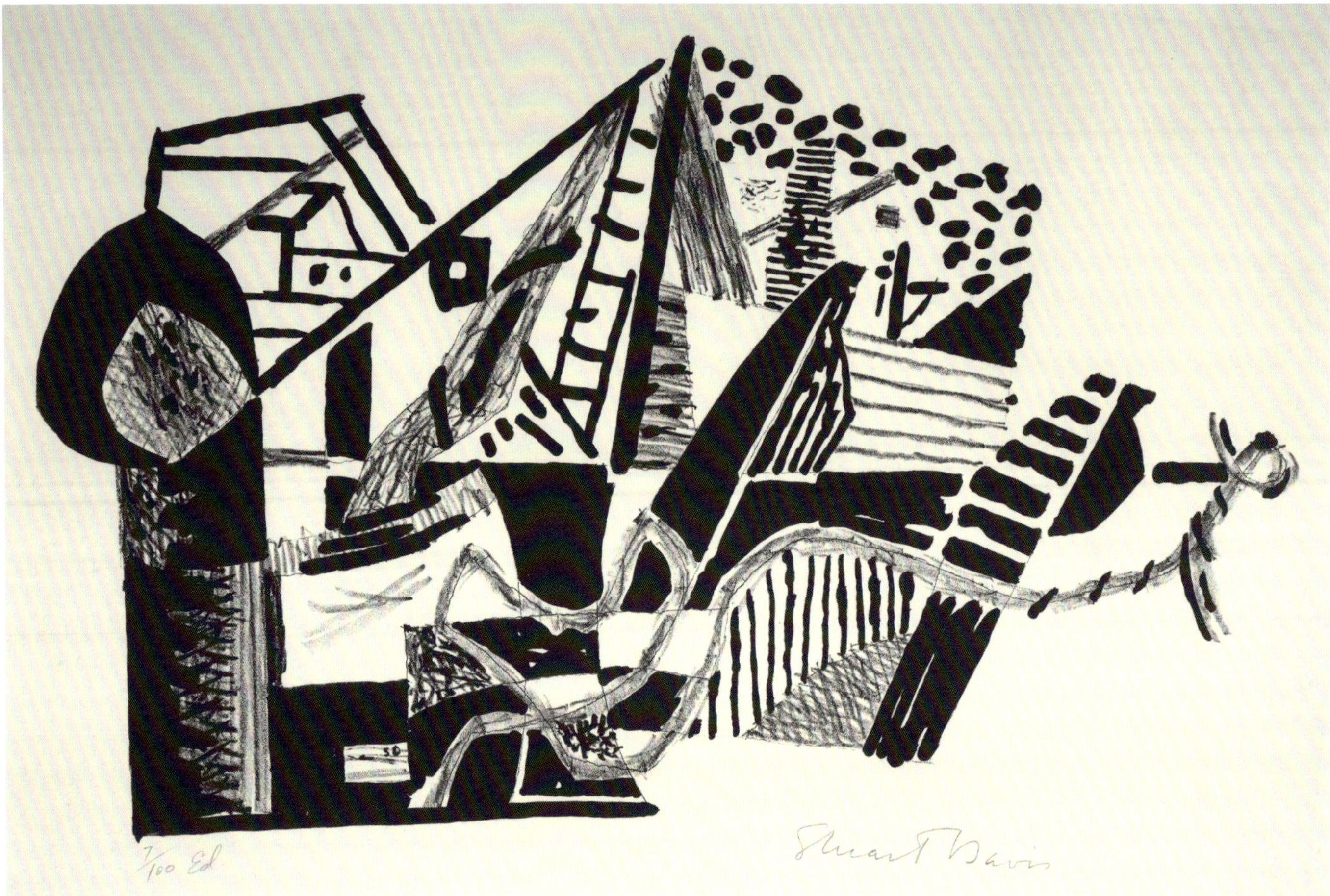

14
Stuart Davis
American, 1892–1964
Anchor, 1936
Lithograph, 11 ¼ × 16

15
Adolf Arthur Dehn
American, 1895–1968
The Great God Pan, 1940
Screenprint on cream wove paper,
9 ⅞ × 13 ½

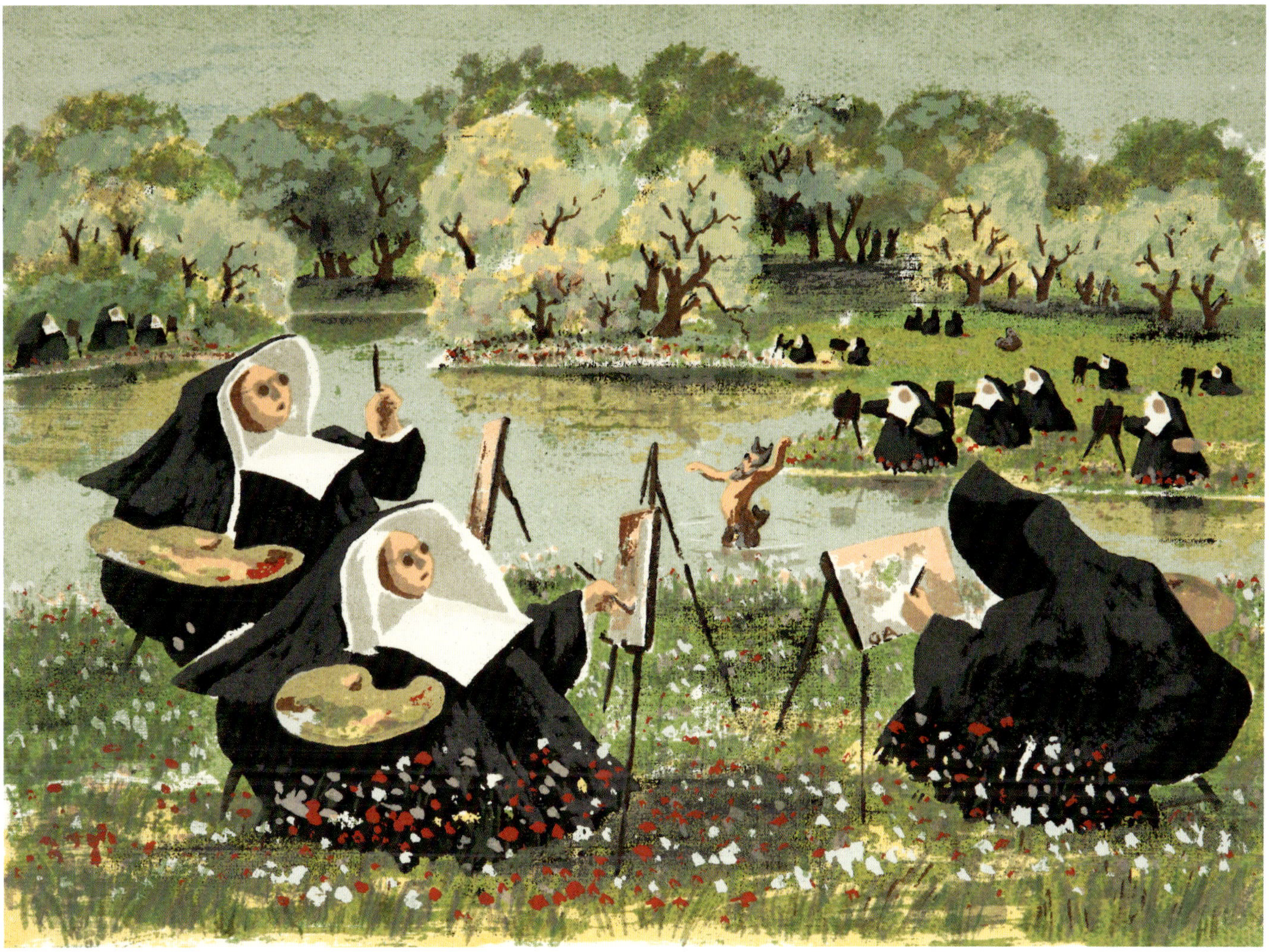

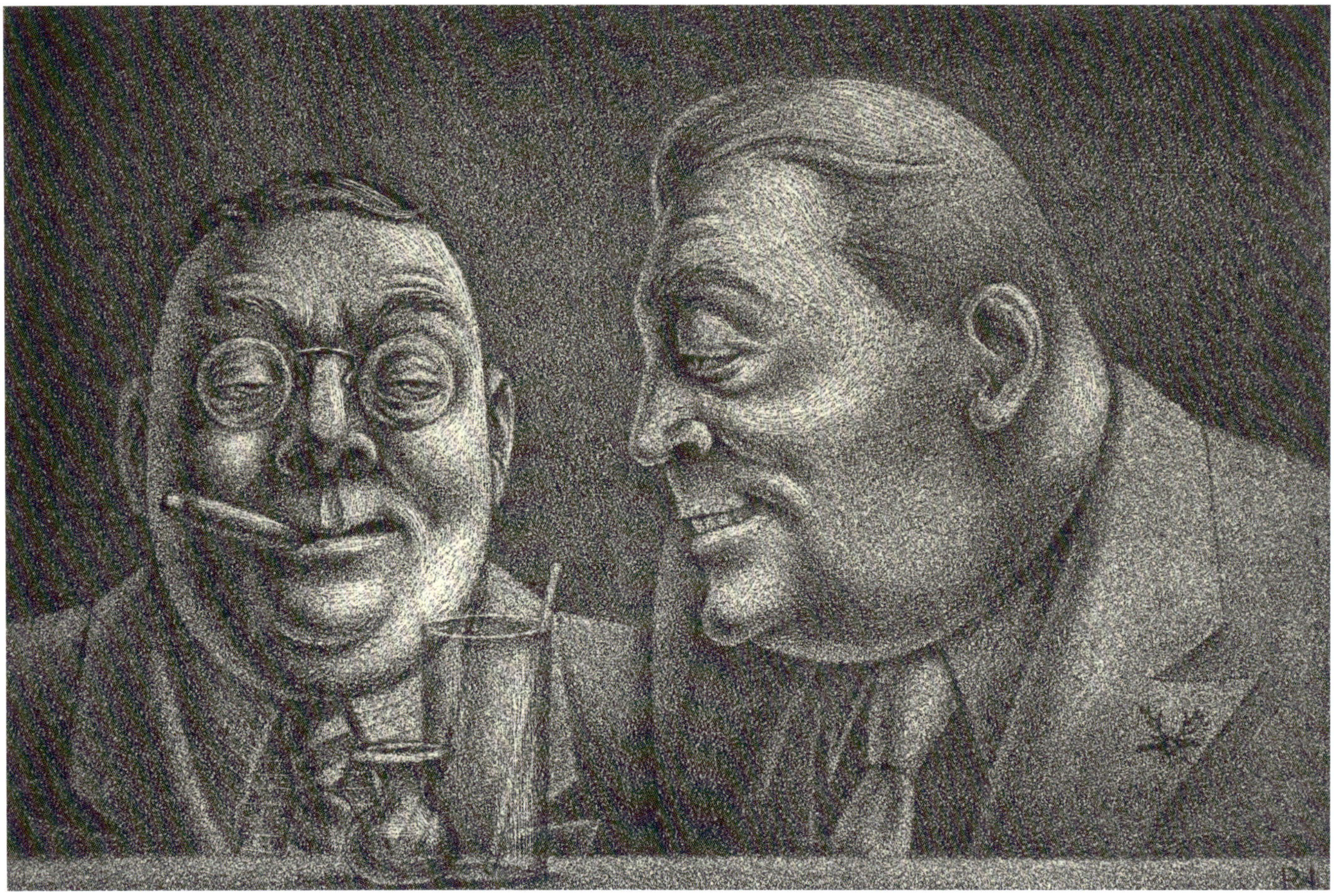

16
Pele deLappe
American, 1916–2007
Big Business, 1937
Lithograph on white wove paper, $6\frac{7}{16} \times 9\frac{7}{8}$

17
Stevan Dohanos
American, 1907–1994
Industrial Landscape, 1935
Wood engraving on cream wove paper, 8 × 10

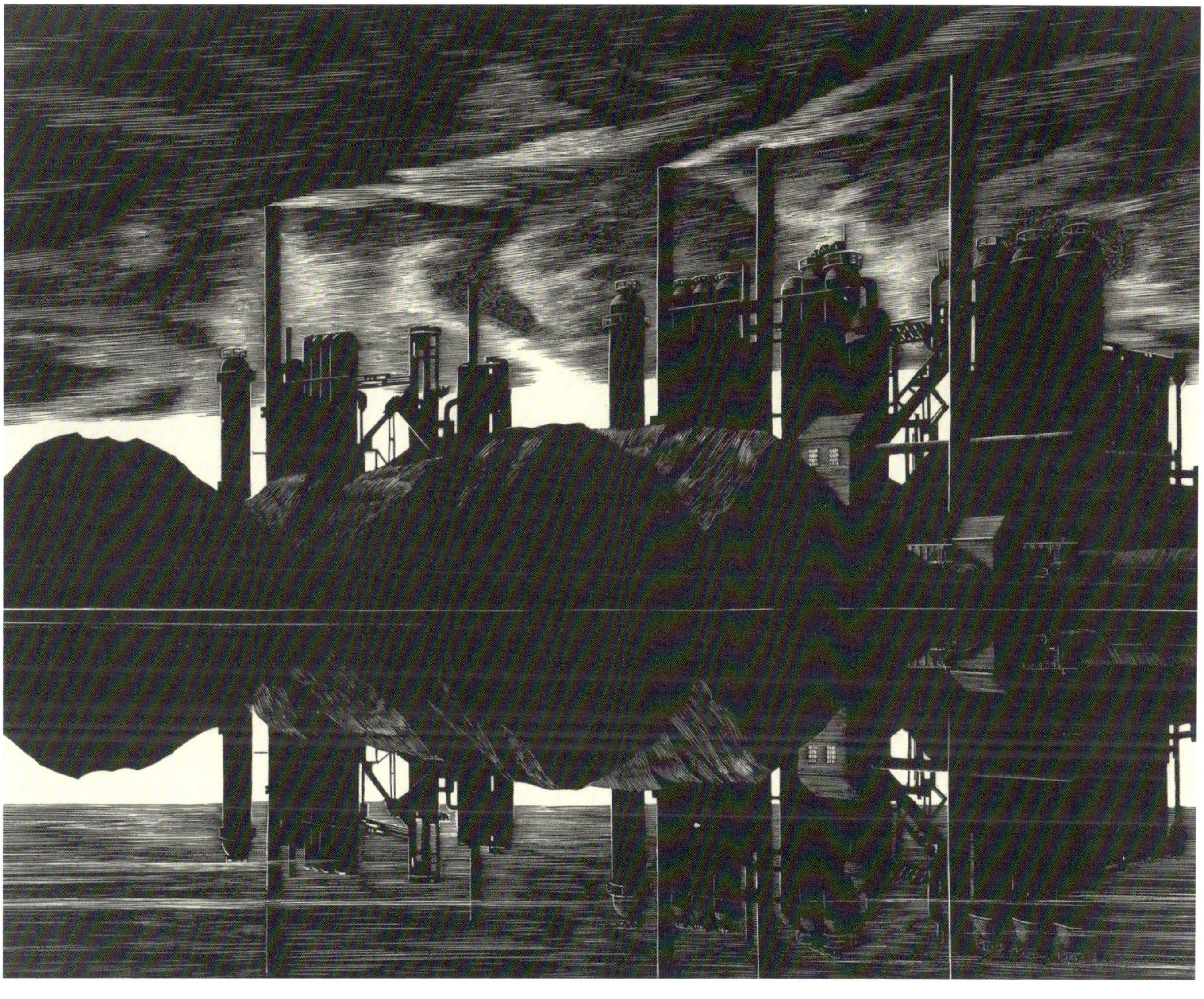

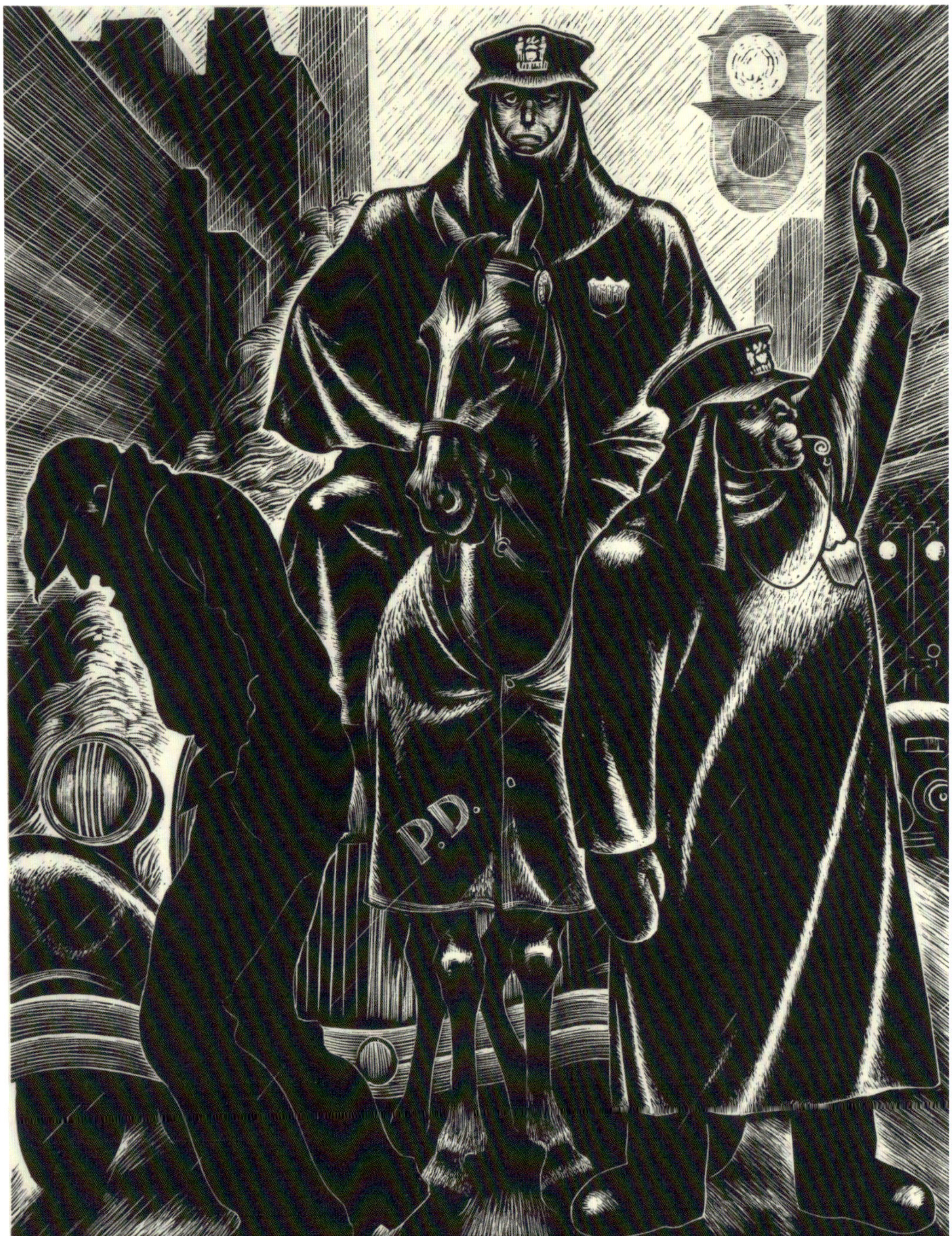
P.D.
Eichenberg

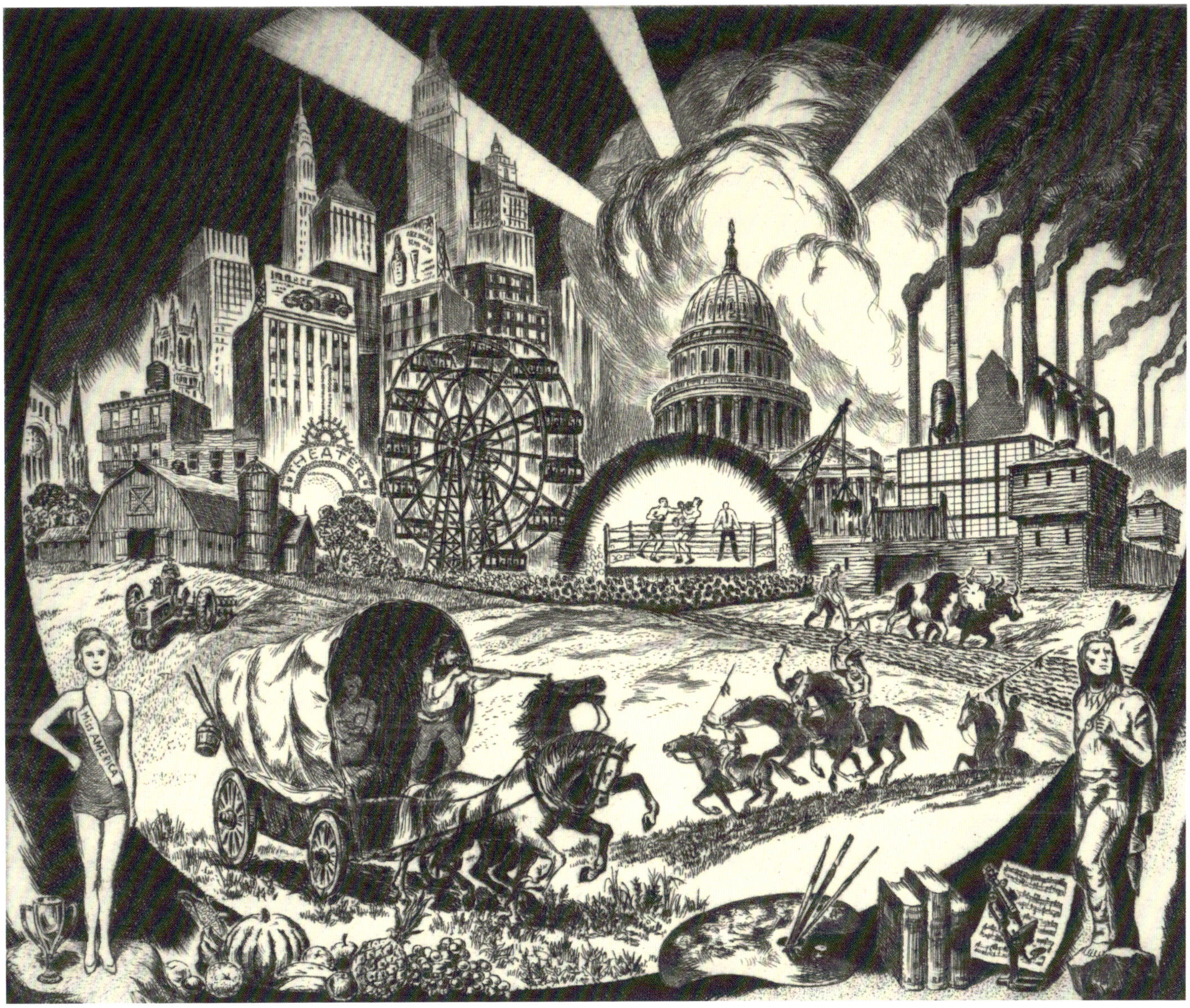

18
Fritz Eichenberg
American, 1901–1990
April Showers, 1935
Wood engraving, $7\frac{1}{4} \times 6$

19
Ralph Fabri
American, 1884–1975
Americana, 1940
Etching, $7\frac{15}{16} \times 9\frac{5}{8}$

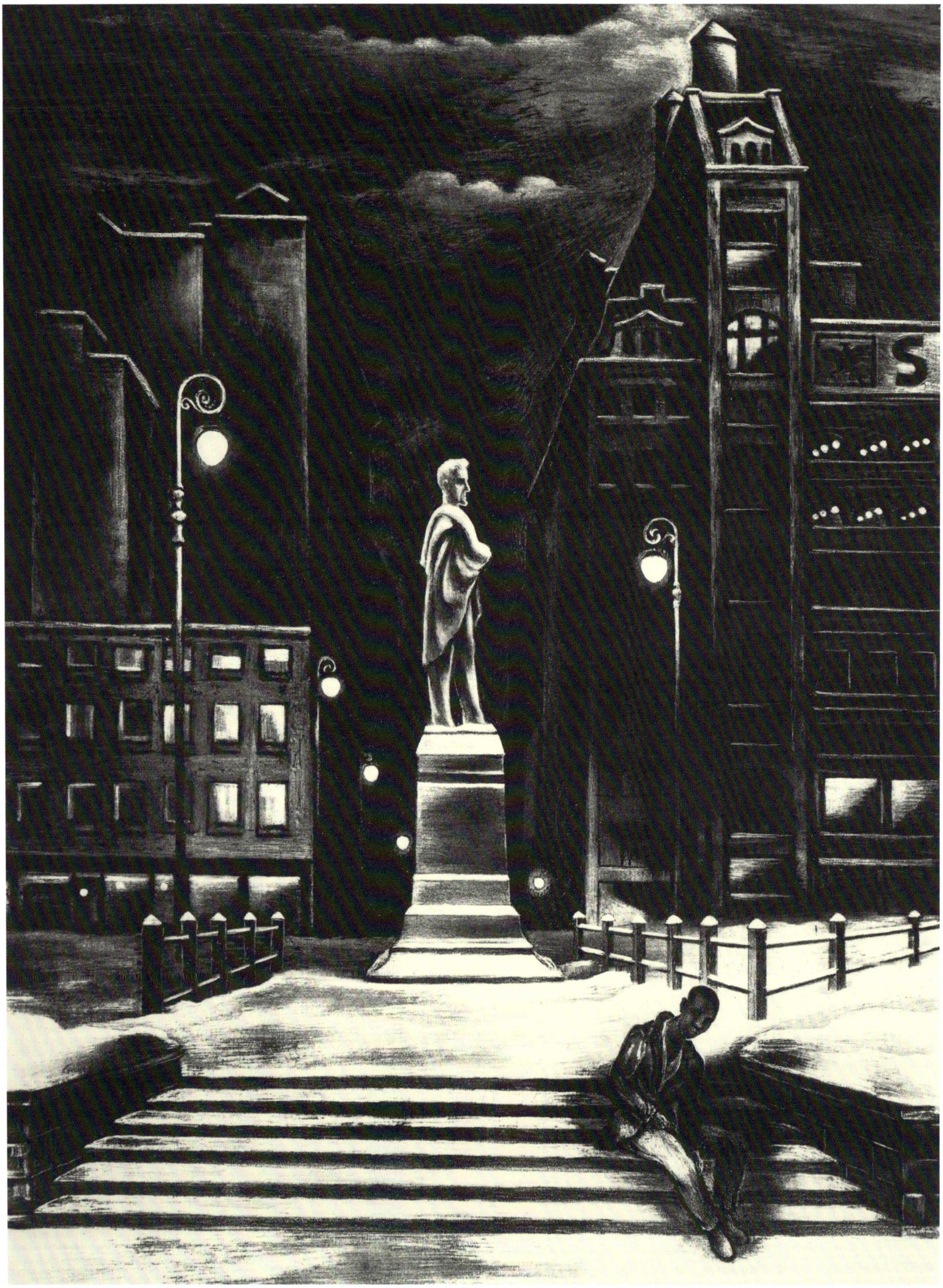
S

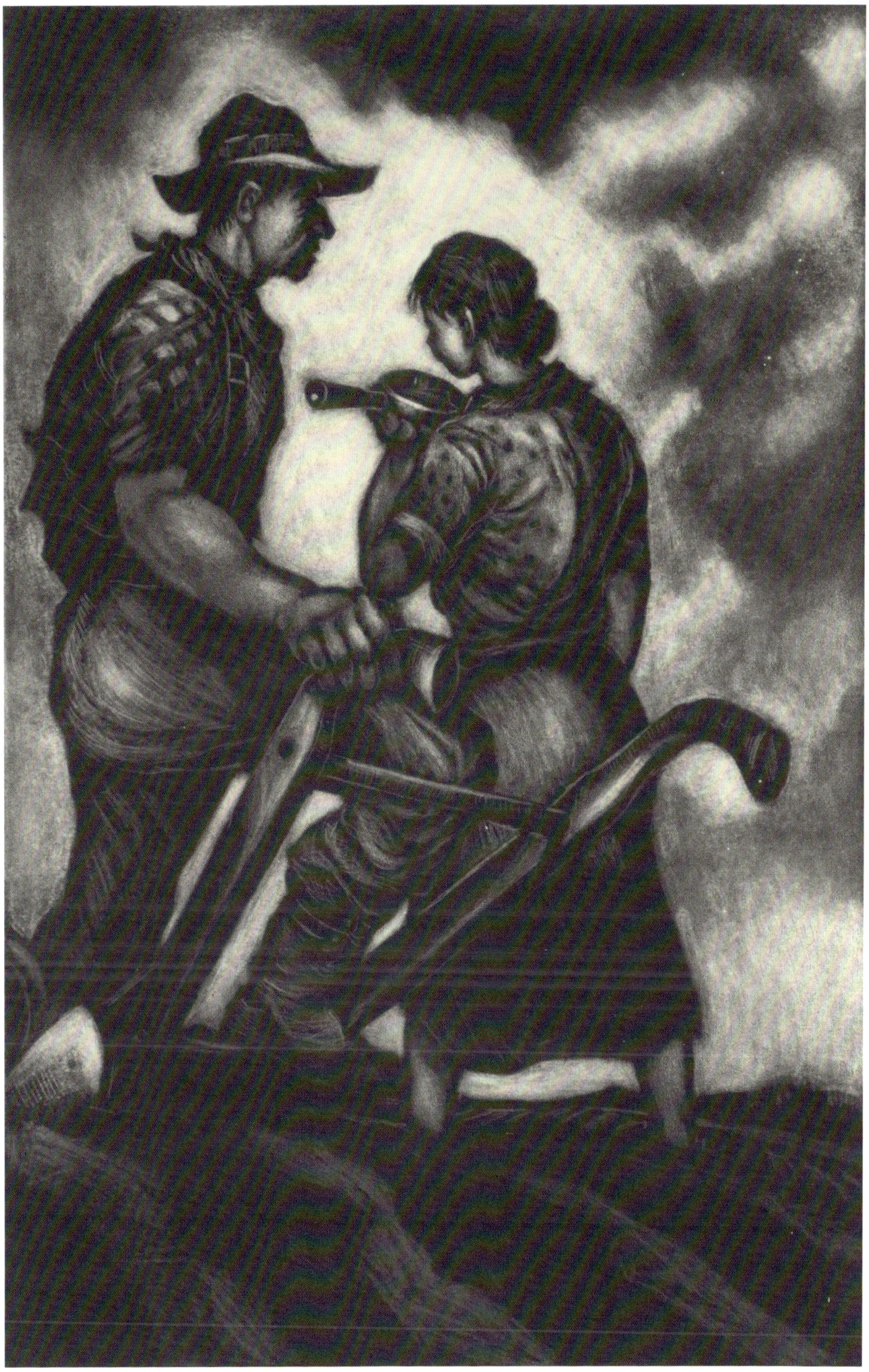

20
Ernest Fiene
American, 1894–1965
Lincoln Monument in Union Square,
1935–1936
Lithograph, 13 3/4 x 10 1/2

21
Michael John Gallagher
American, 1898–1965
Toilers, 1940
Carborundum, 12 7/8 x 8 1/2

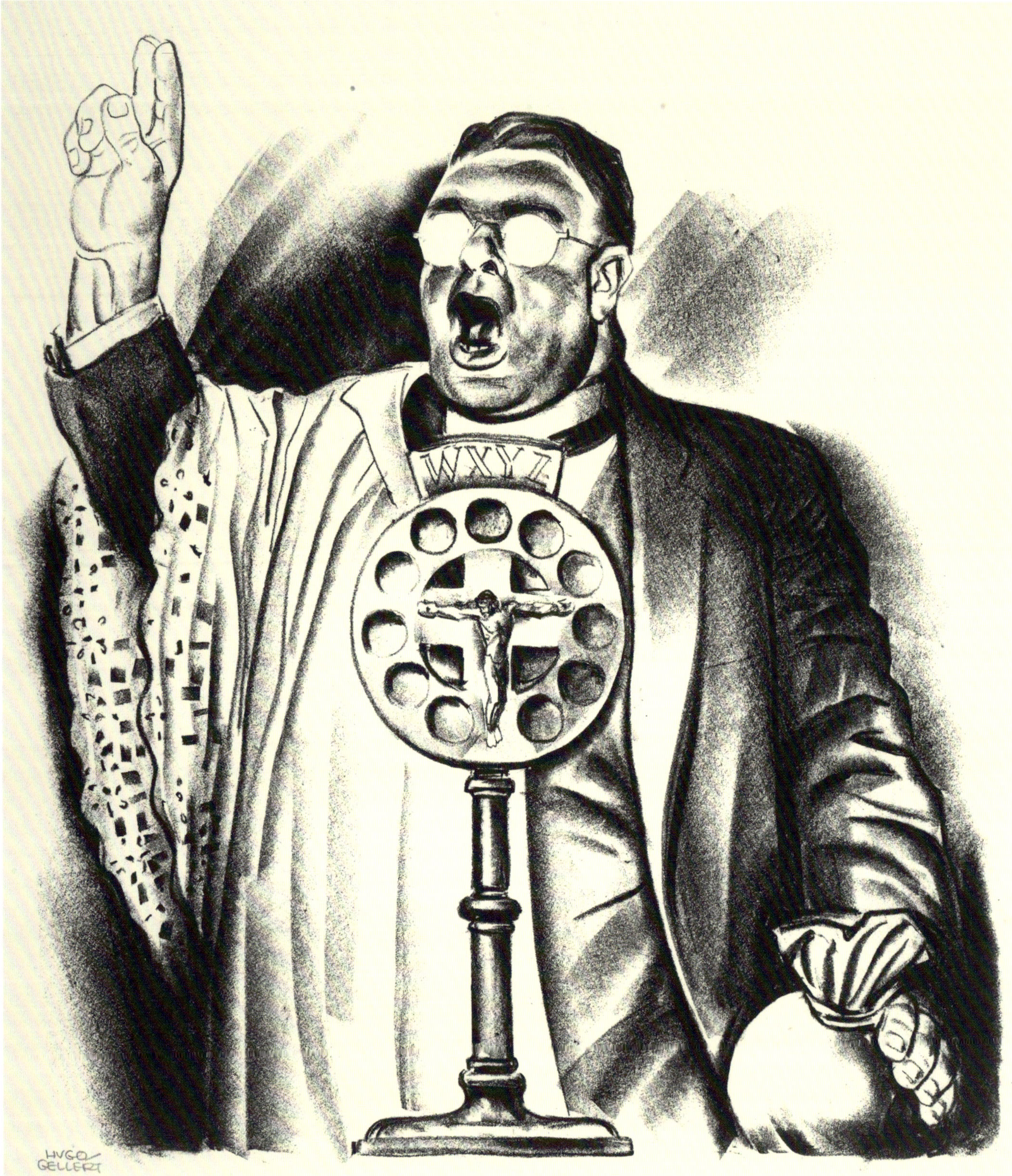
WXYZ
HUGO GELLERT

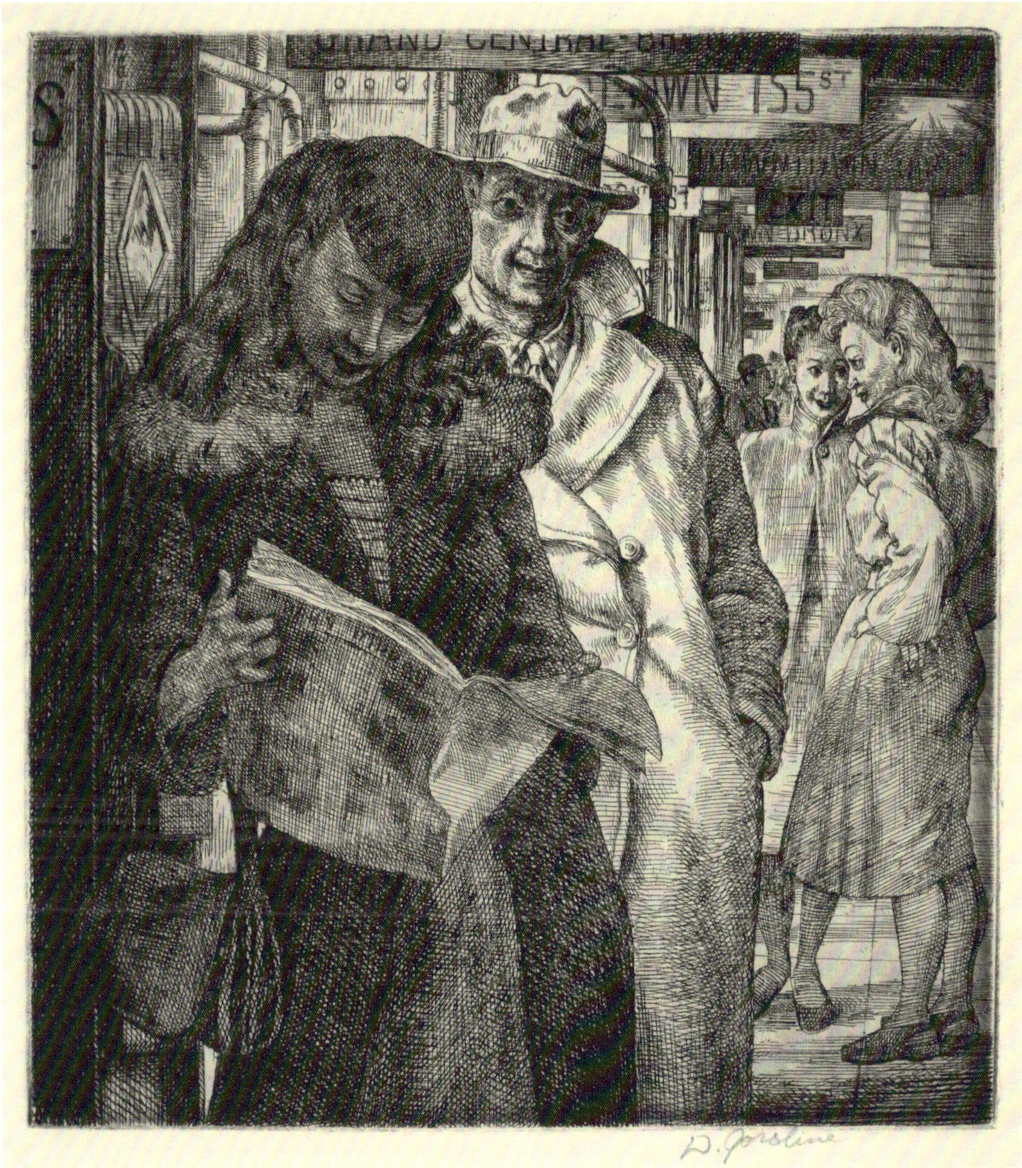

22
Hugo Gellert
American, 1892–1985
Father Coughlin and His Flock, 1936
Lithograph on ivory wove paper,
12⅝ x 11⅝

23
Douglas Warner Gorsline
American, 1913–1985
Express Stop, 1945
Etching on cream wove paper,
6¼ x 5¾

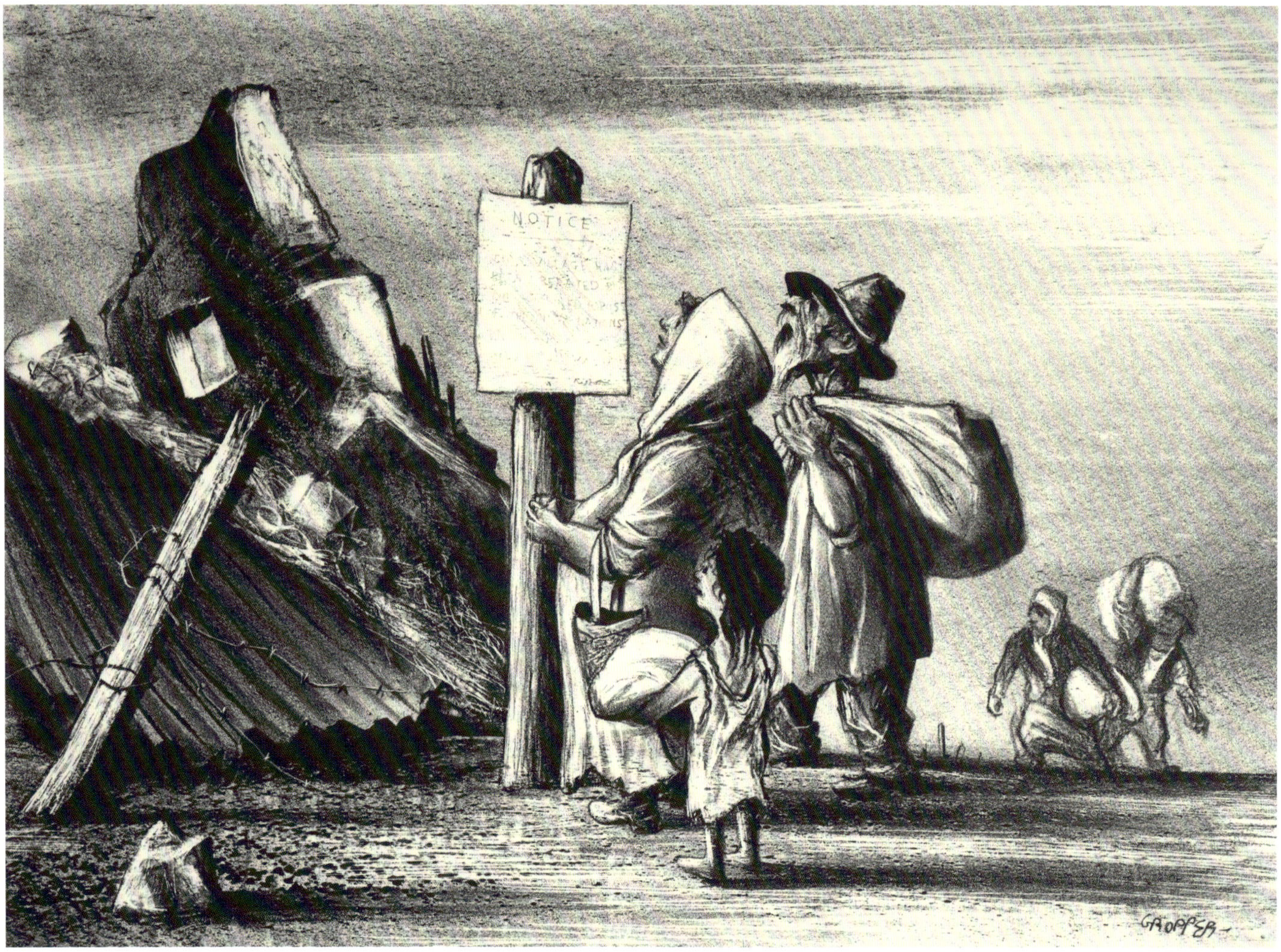

24
William Gropper
American, 1897–1977
Liberated Village, 1939
Lithograph on ivory wove paper,
12 × 16¾

25
Harold Maxwell Hahn
American, 1920–2012
Autumn in Mill Street, 1940
Color woodcut on cream japan paper,
12 × 9

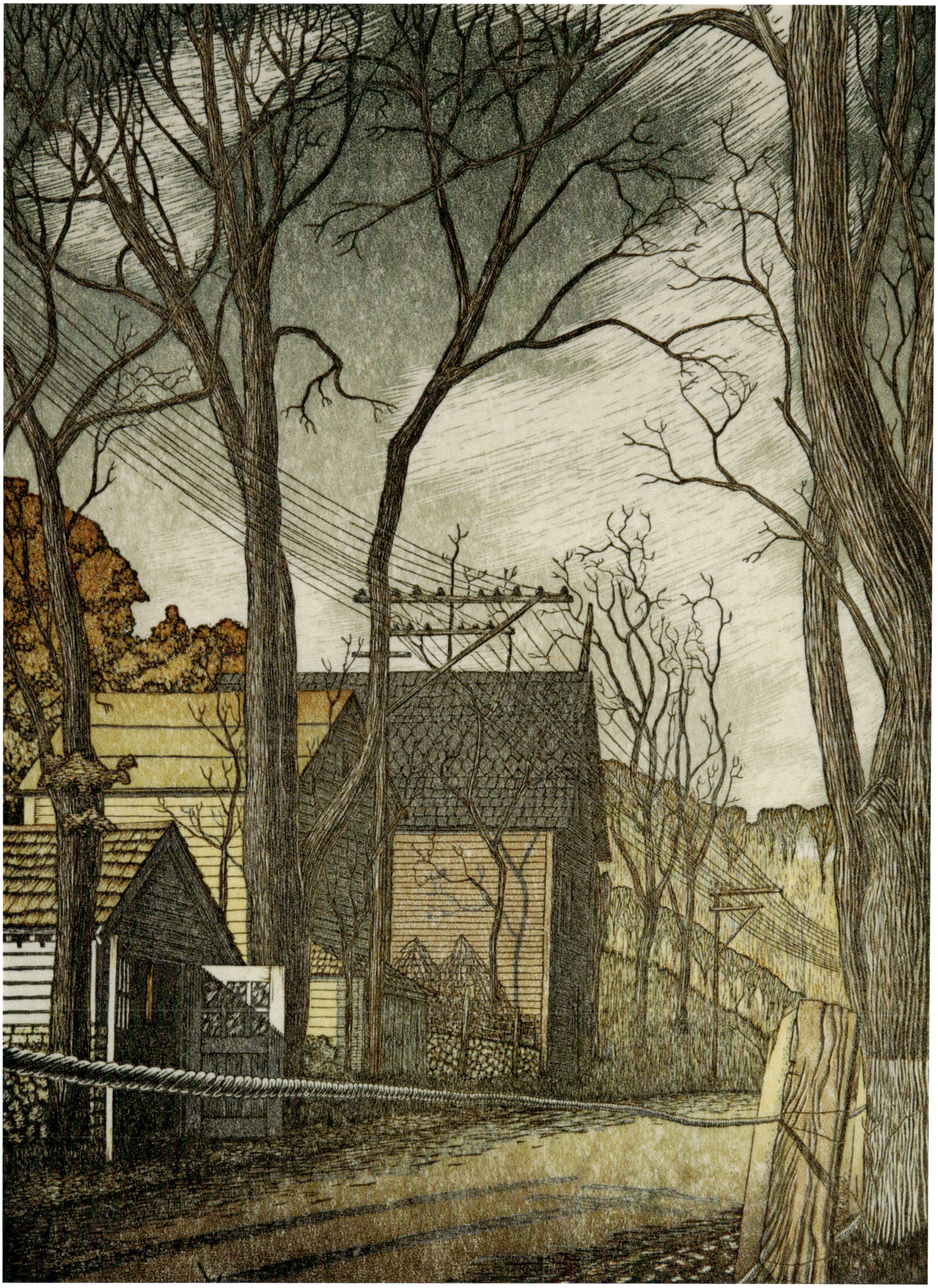

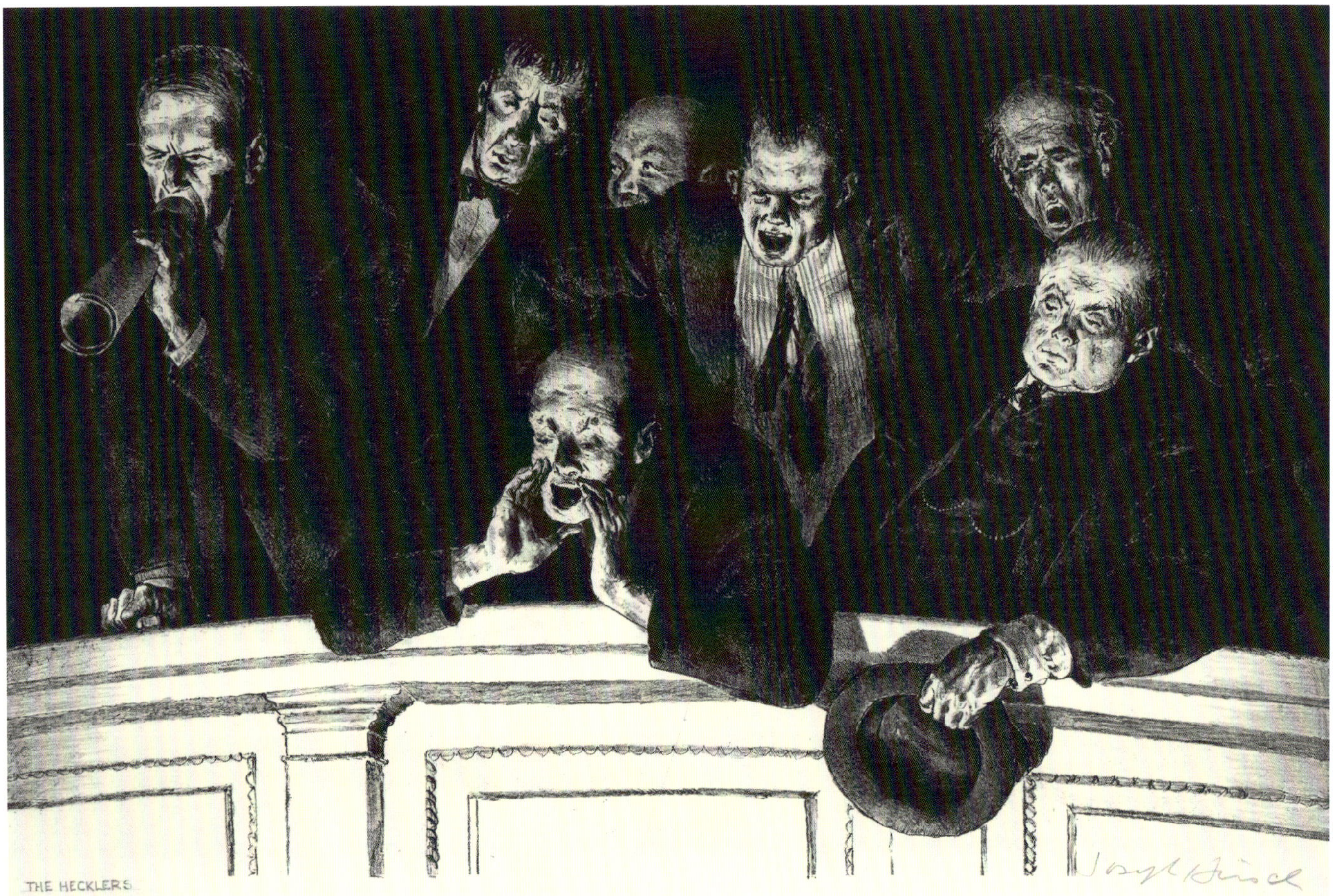

26
Joseph Hirsch
American, 1910–1981
*The Heckler*s, 1943
Lithograph on cream wove paper, 9 ¾ × 15 ¼

27
Charles Keller
American, 1914–2006
Fighter for Democracy, 1942
Nine-color screenprint on cream wove paper, 12 ⅛ × 17 ¼

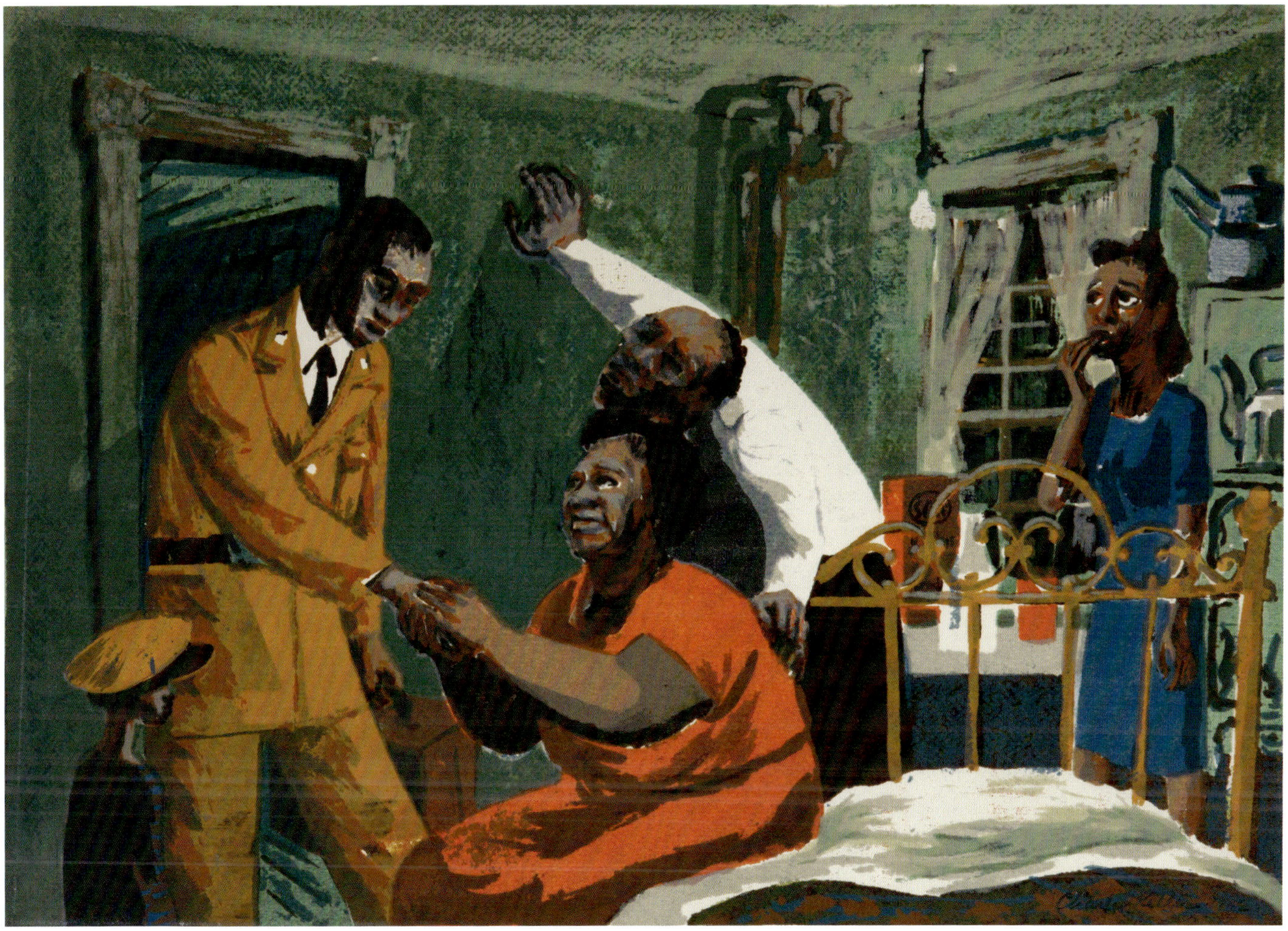

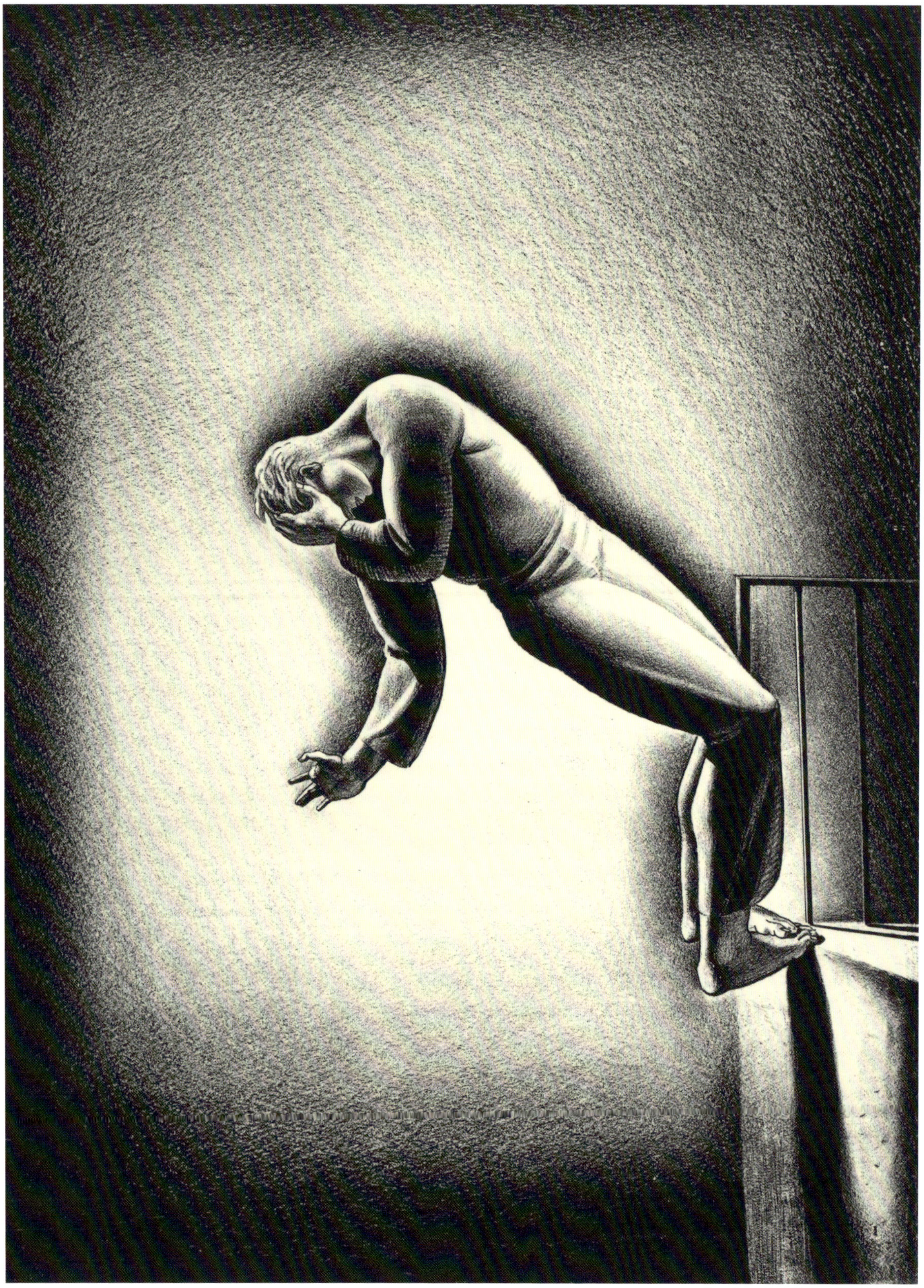

28
Rockwell Kent
American, 1882–1971
Nightmare, 1941
Lithograph on ivory wove paper,
10 7/8 × 8 1/16

29
Clayton Knight
American, 1891–1969
The Last Lap, 1940
Lithograph on ivory wove paper,
12 5/8 × 9 5/8

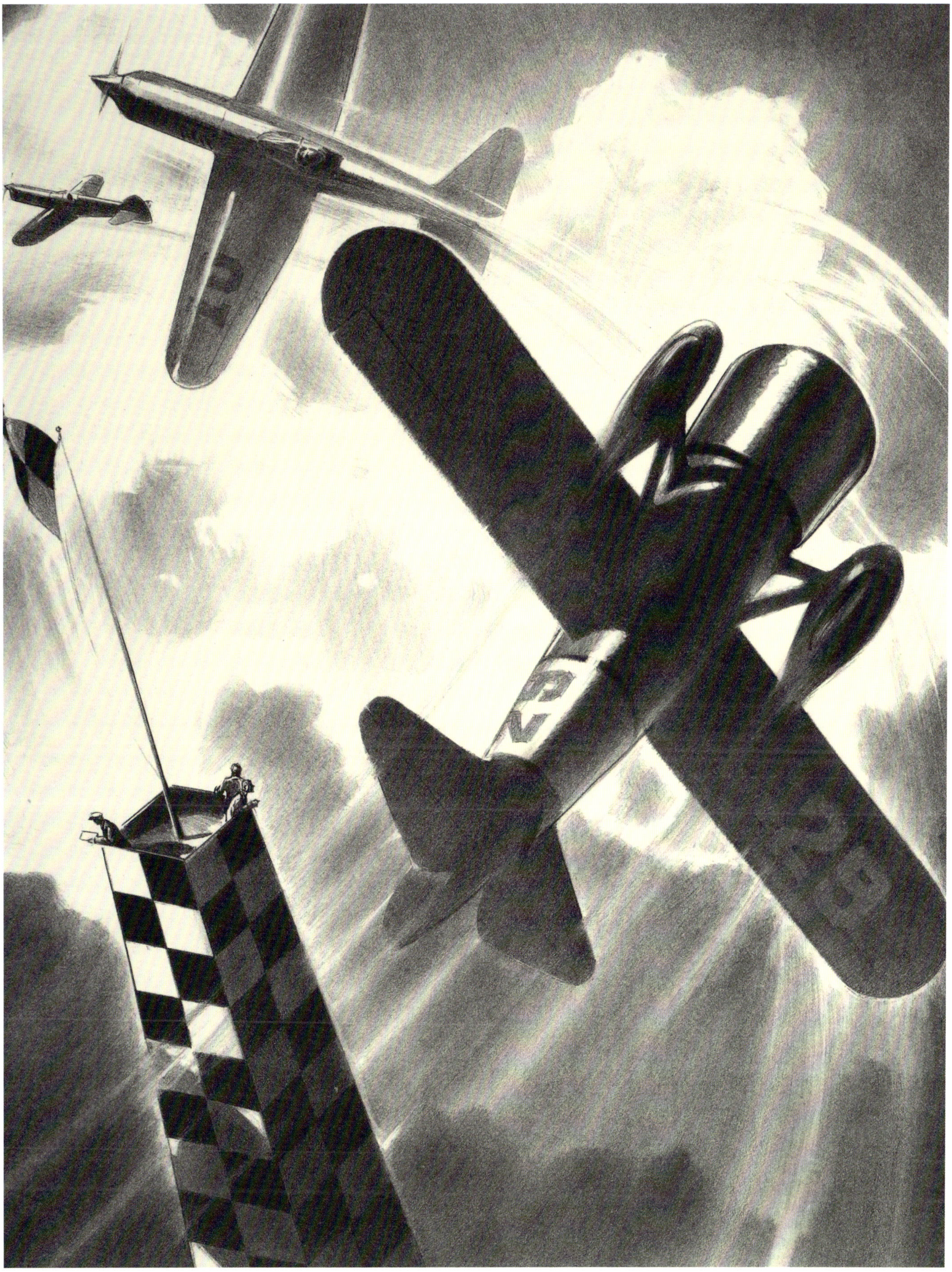

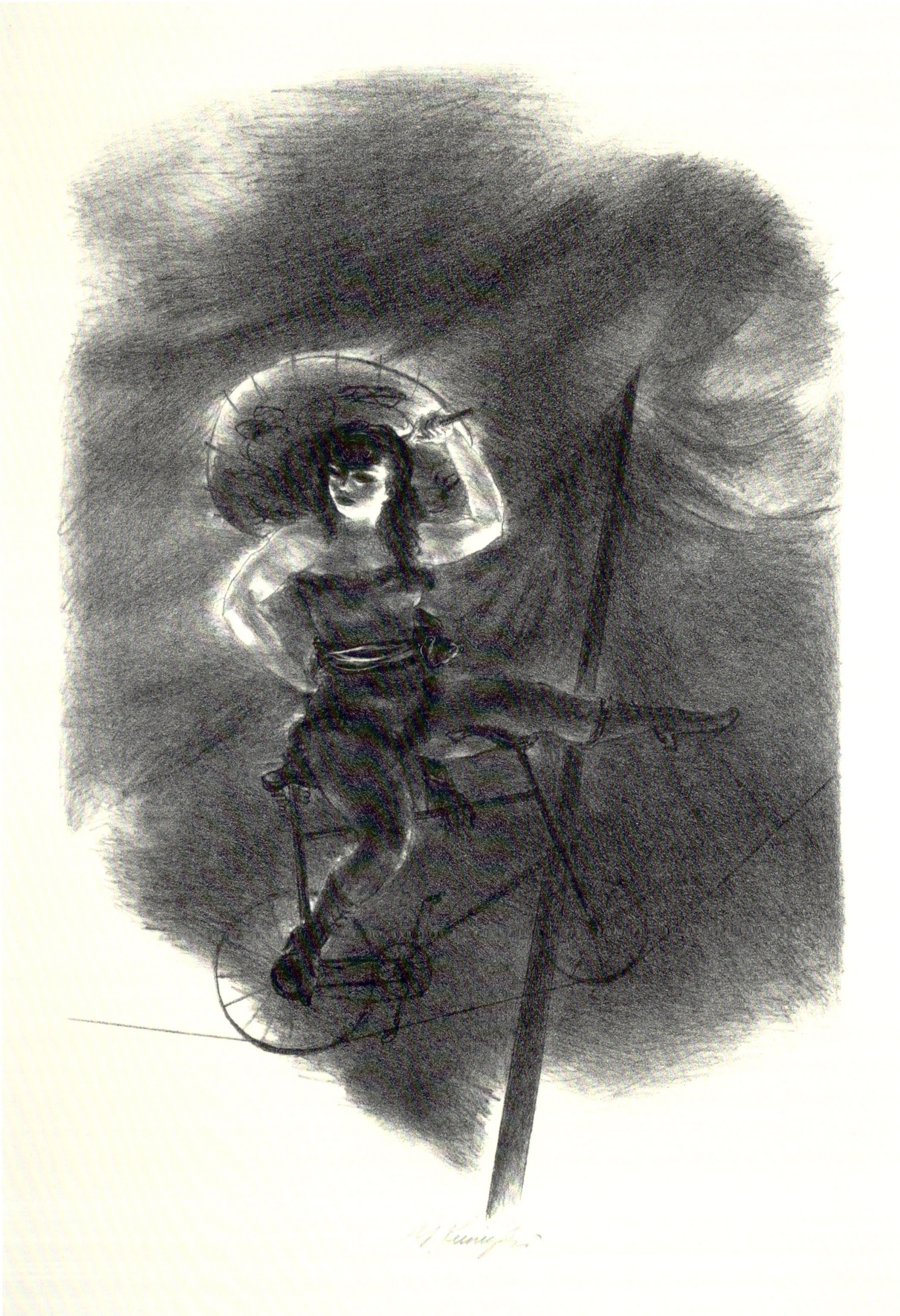

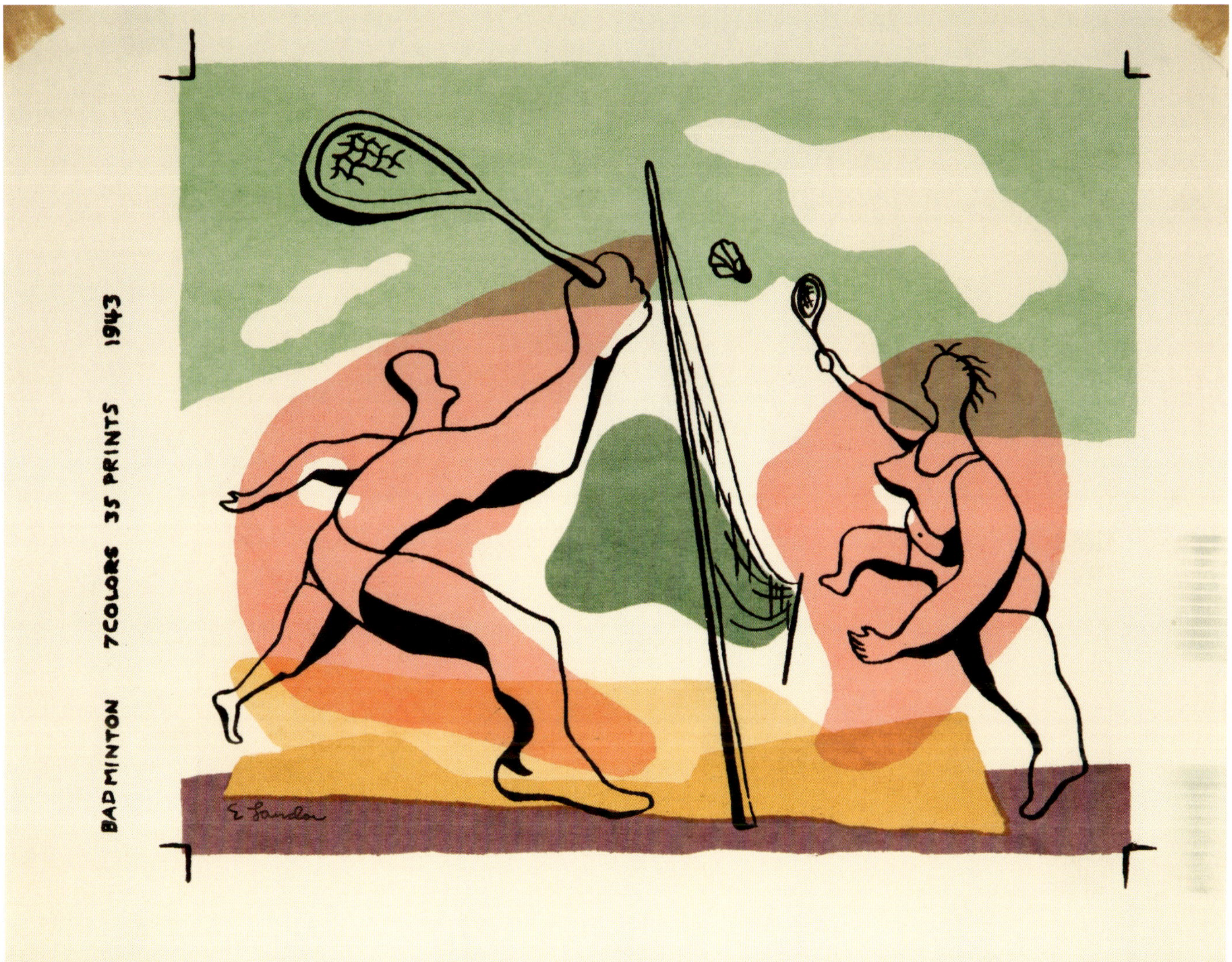

30
Yasuo Kuniyoshi
American, born Japan, 1893–1953
Cyclist, 1939
Lithograph on cream wove paper,
16 7/8 × 12 1/2

31
Edward August Landon
American, 1911–1984
Badminton, 1943
Screenprint on cream wove paper,
8 3/16 × 10 1/8

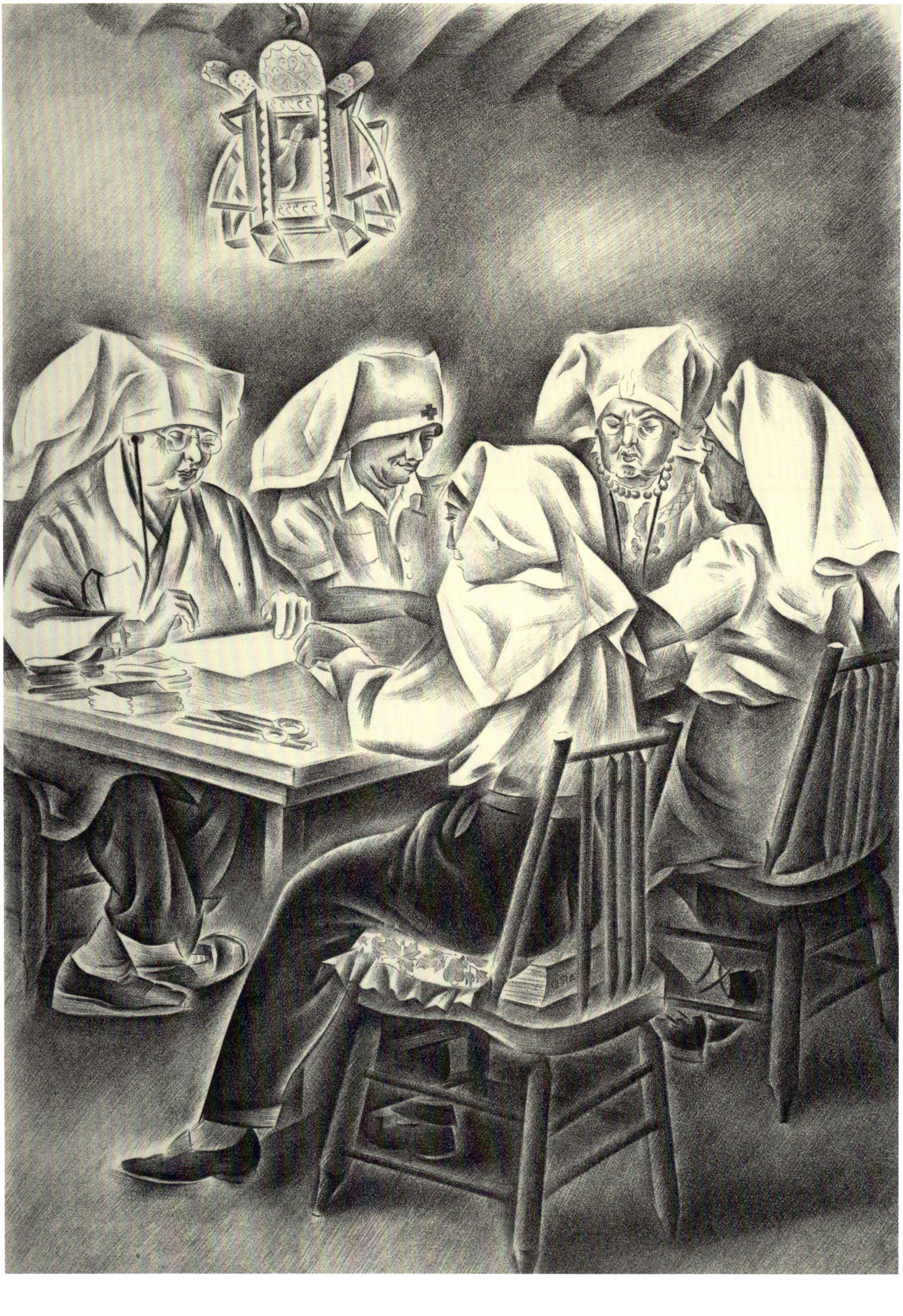

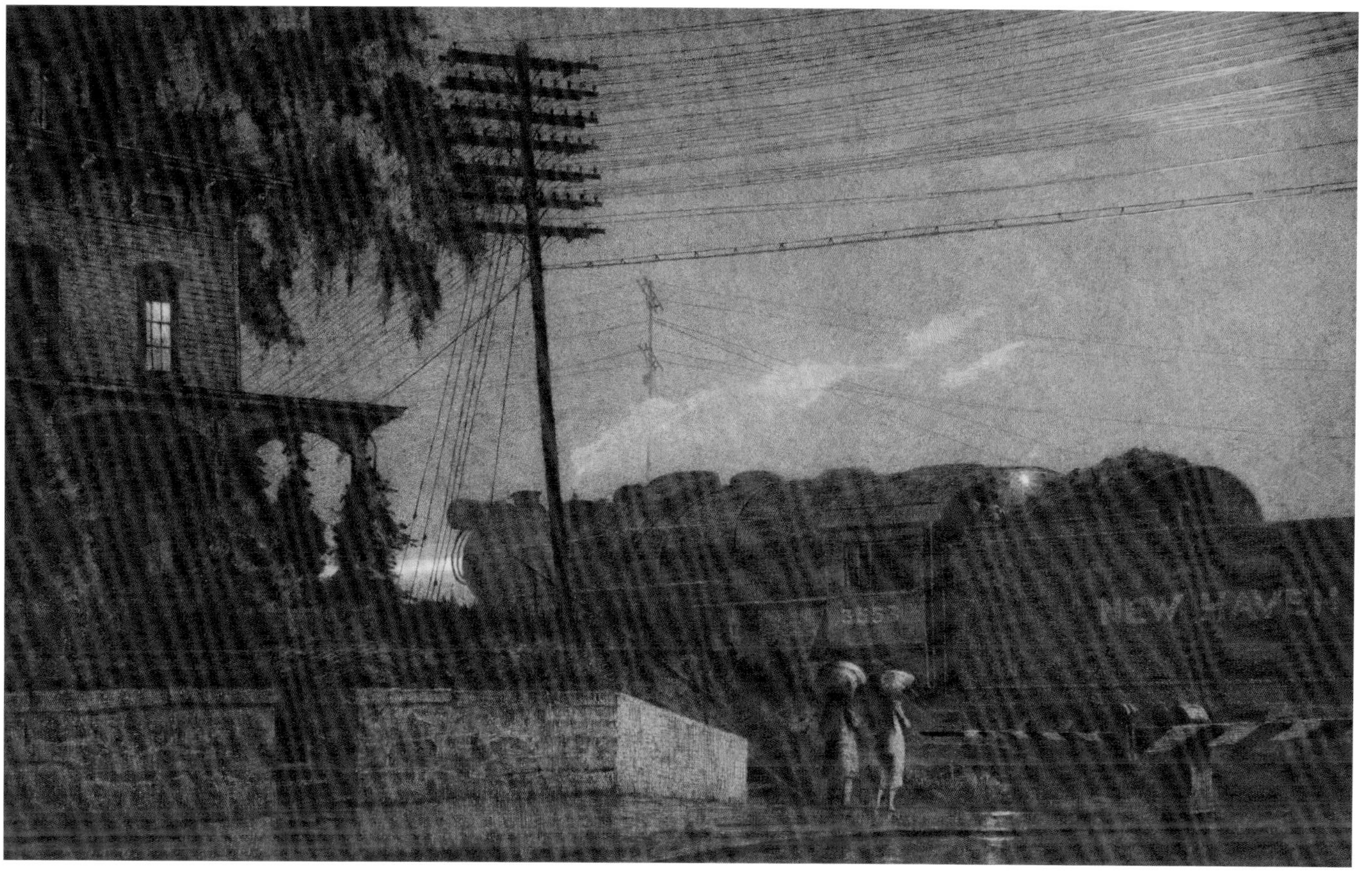

32
Barbara Latham
American, 1896–1989
Our Chapter (Taos), 1943
Lithograph on cream wove paper,
$14\frac{3}{4} \times 10\frac{3}{4}$

33
Martin Lewis
American, 1881–1962
Passing Freight, 1938
Drypoint on ivory wove paper,
$8\frac{7}{8} \times 14\frac{1}{4}$

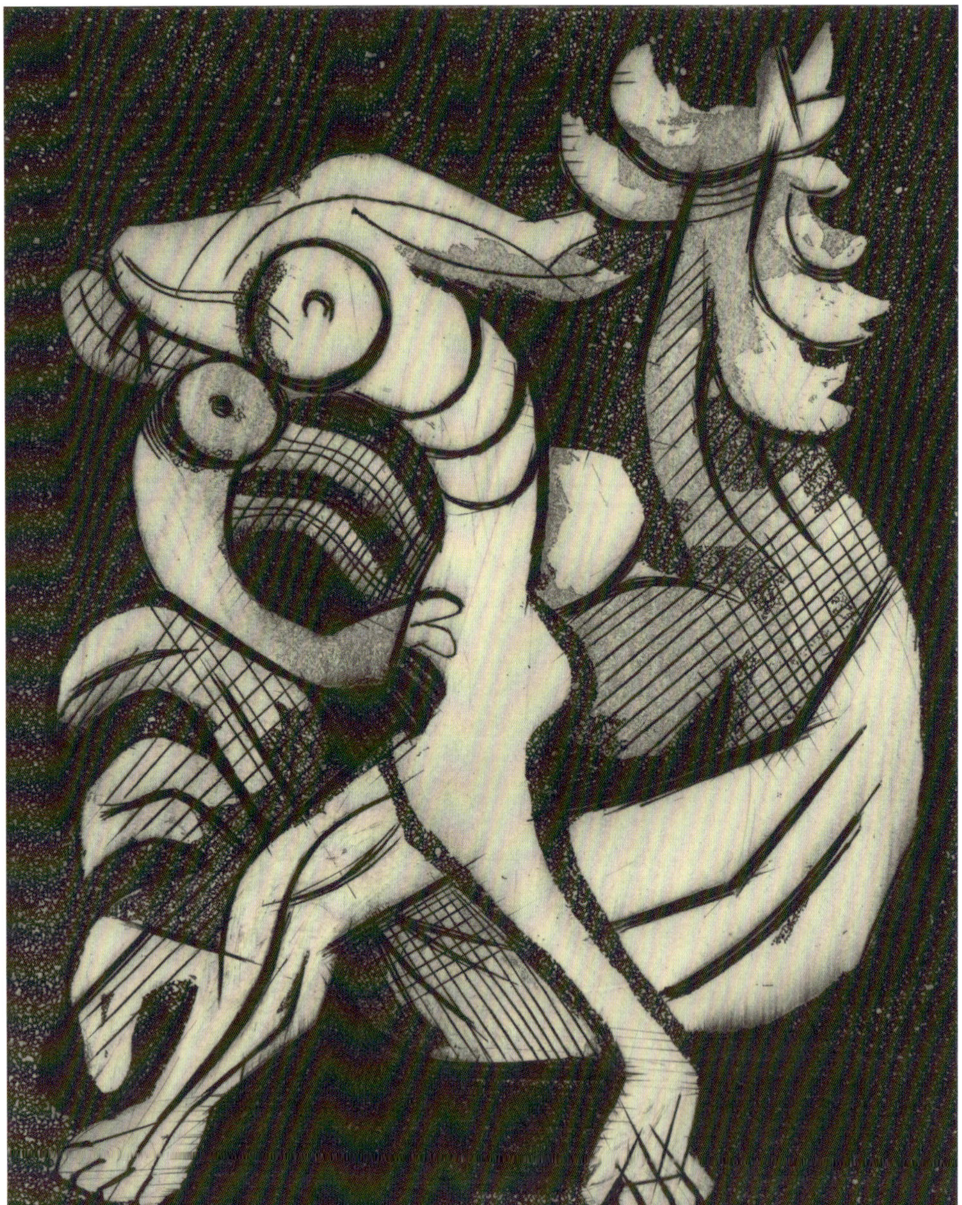

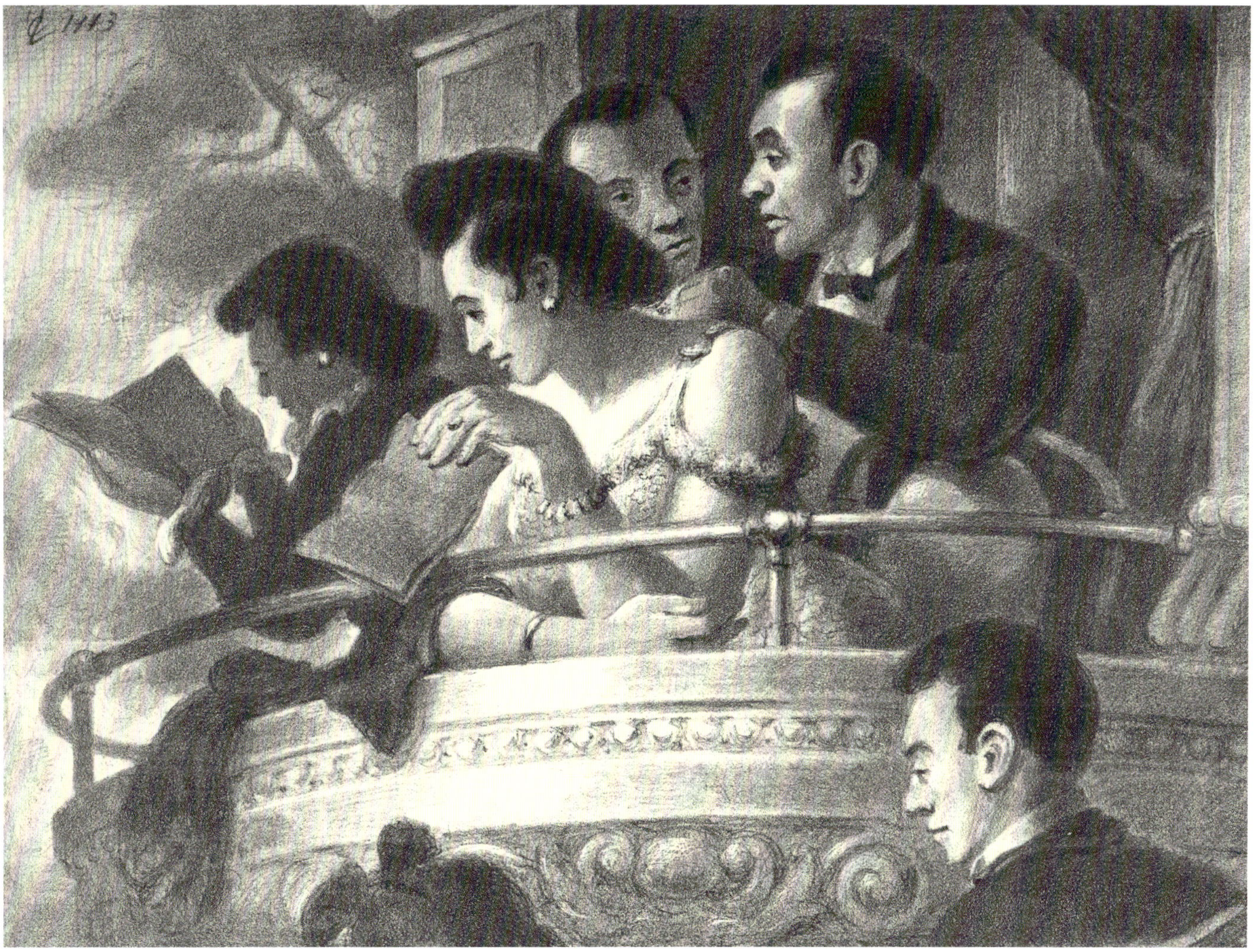

34
Jacques Lipchitz
American, 1891–1973
Danseuse et coq (Dancer and Cockerel), 1940
Etching, aquatint, engraving, and drypoint on cream wove paper,
$6\frac{7}{8} \times 5\frac{7}{16}$

35
Charles Wheeler Locke
American, 1899–1983
The Box, 1943
Lithograph on ivory wove paper,
$9\frac{7}{8} \times 13\frac{3}{8}$

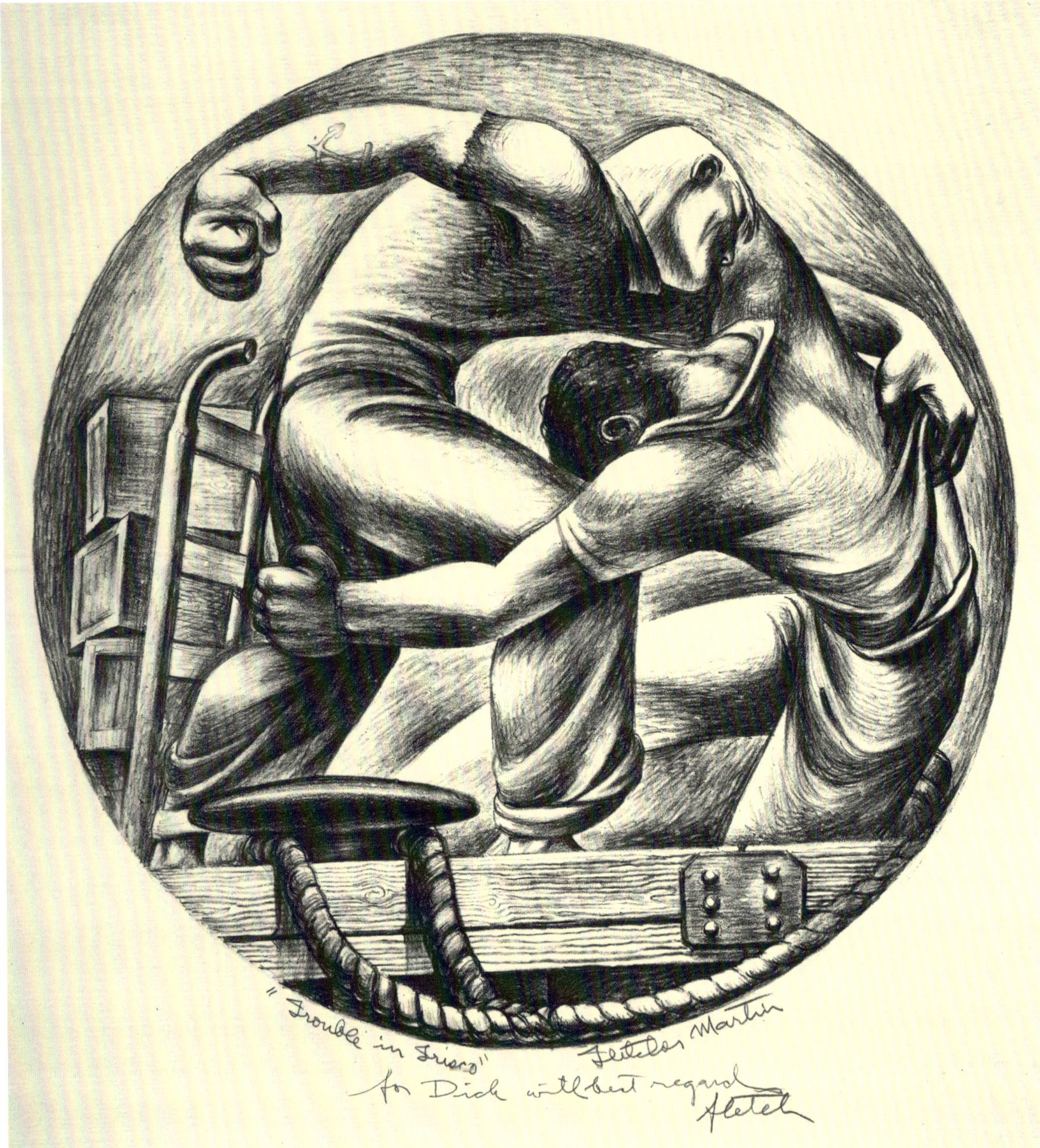

36
Fletcher Martin
American, 1904–1979
Trouble in Frisco, 1938
Lithograph on cream paper,
11 1/16 (diameter)

37
Alice Trumbull Mason
American, 1904–1971
Untitled, from the *American Abstract Artists Portfolio*, 1937
Lithograph on white wove paper,
8 7/8 x 6 1/8

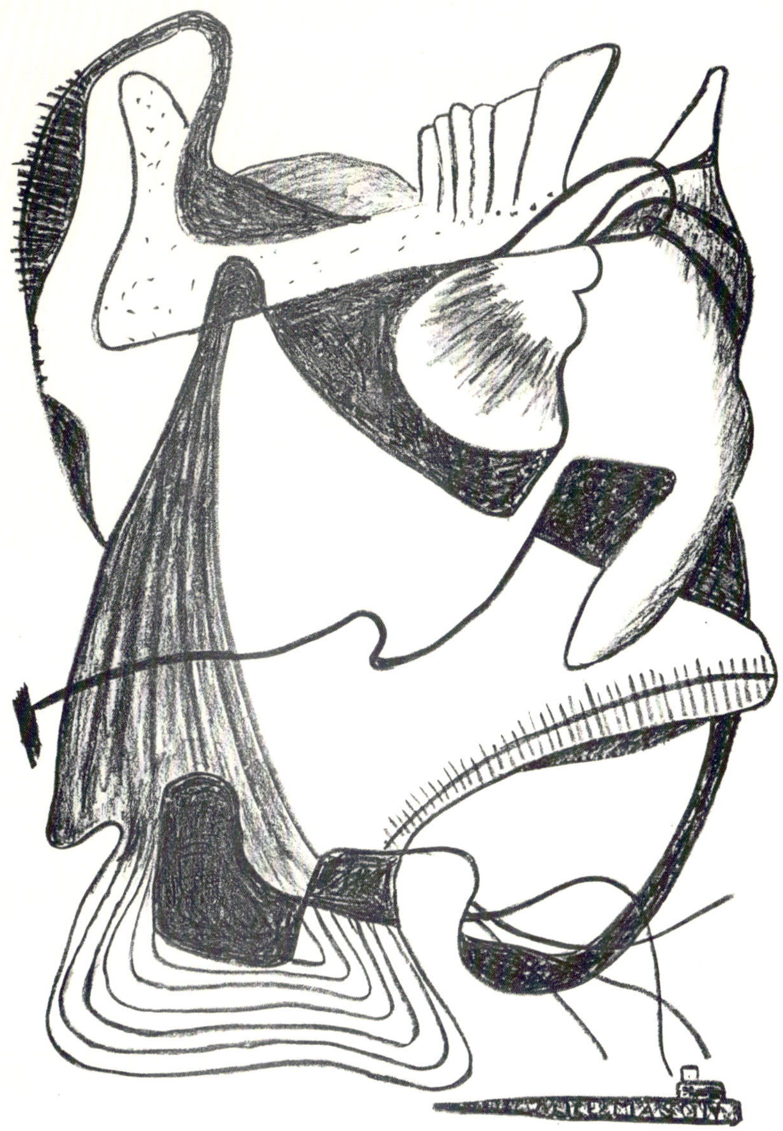

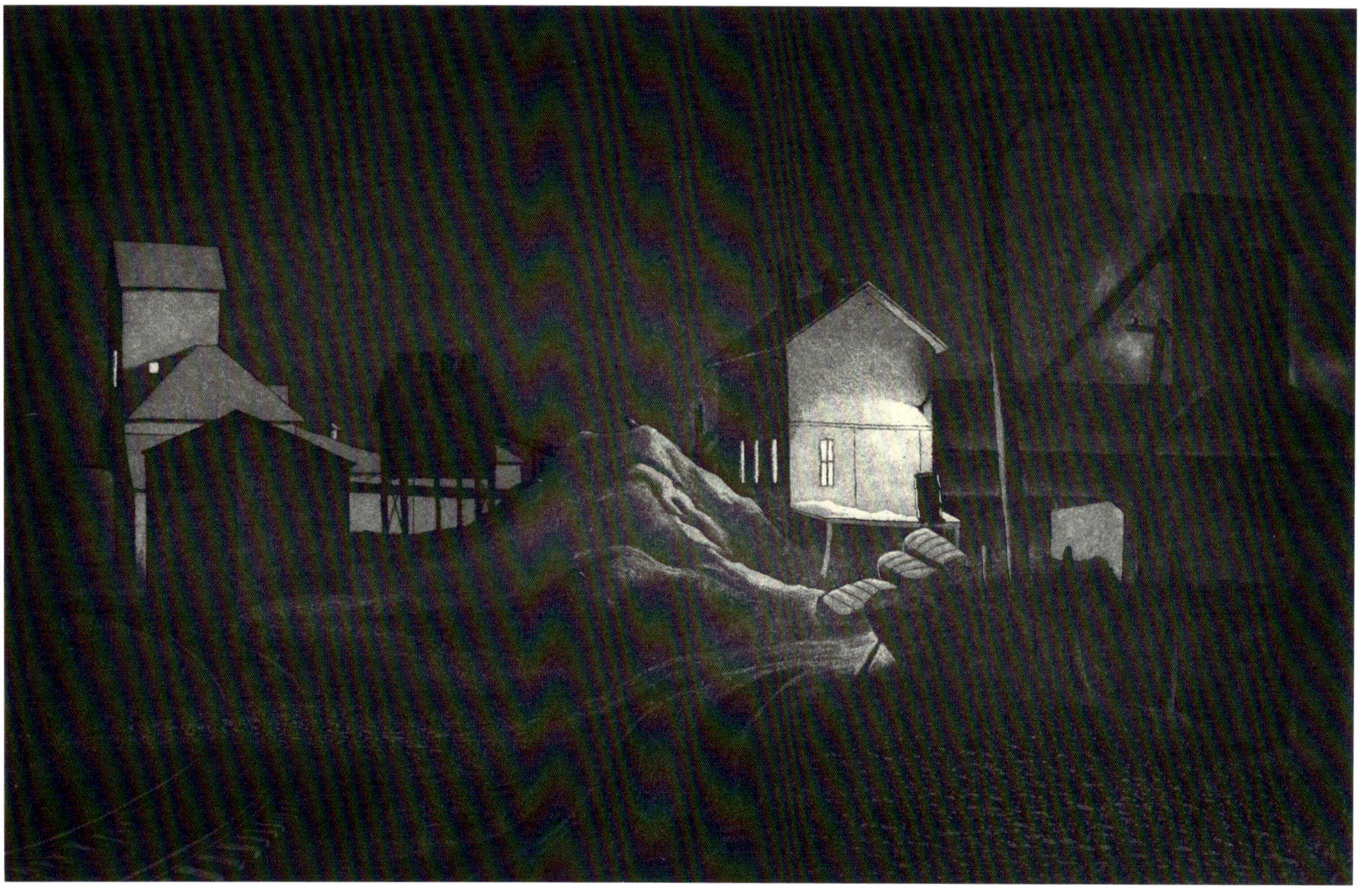

38
J. Jay McVicker
American, 1911–2004
Cotton Gin, 1939
Aquatint on ivory wove paper,
11 3/4 × 17

39
Carl Pickhardt
American, 1908–2004
Tap Dancer, 1938
Lithograph on ivory wove paper,
11 7/8 × 11 1/2

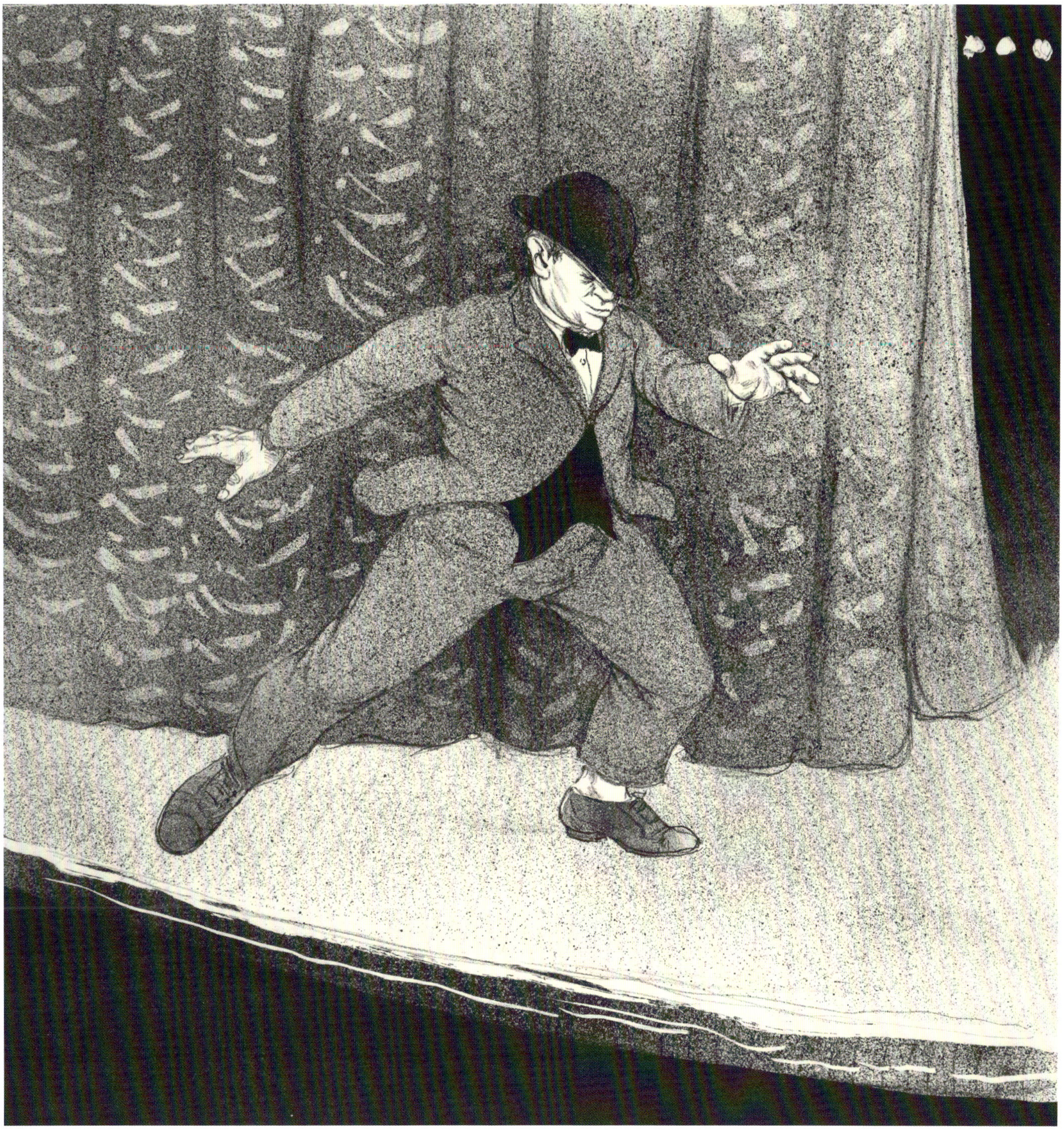

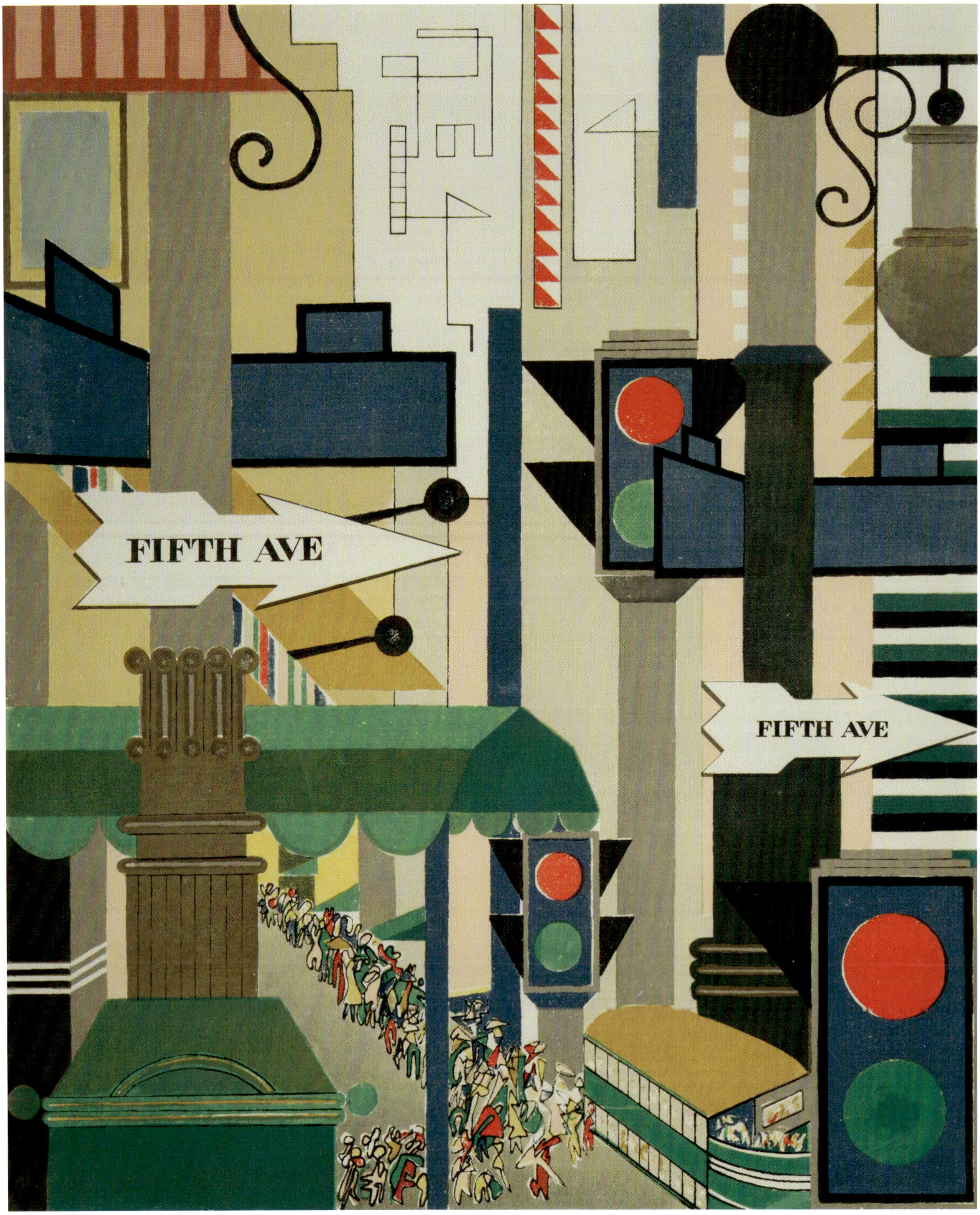
FIFTH AVE
FIFTH AVE

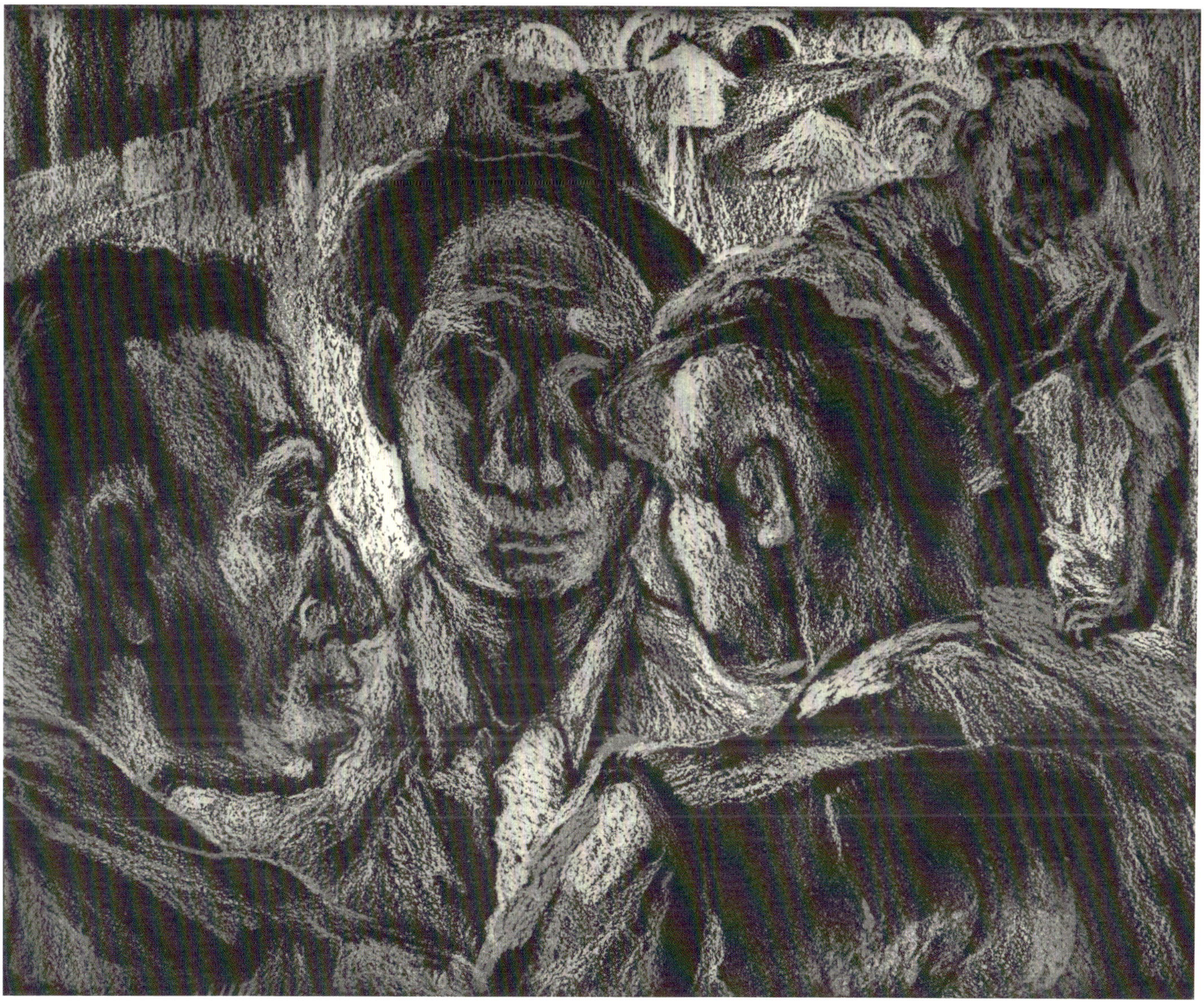

40
Mildred Rackley
American, 1906–1992
Fifth Avenue, 1939–1940
Screenprint on paper, 18 × 15

41
Dorothy Rutka
American, 1907–1985
Strike Talk, 1935
Aquatint on cream wove paper,
6 3/8 × 7 7/8

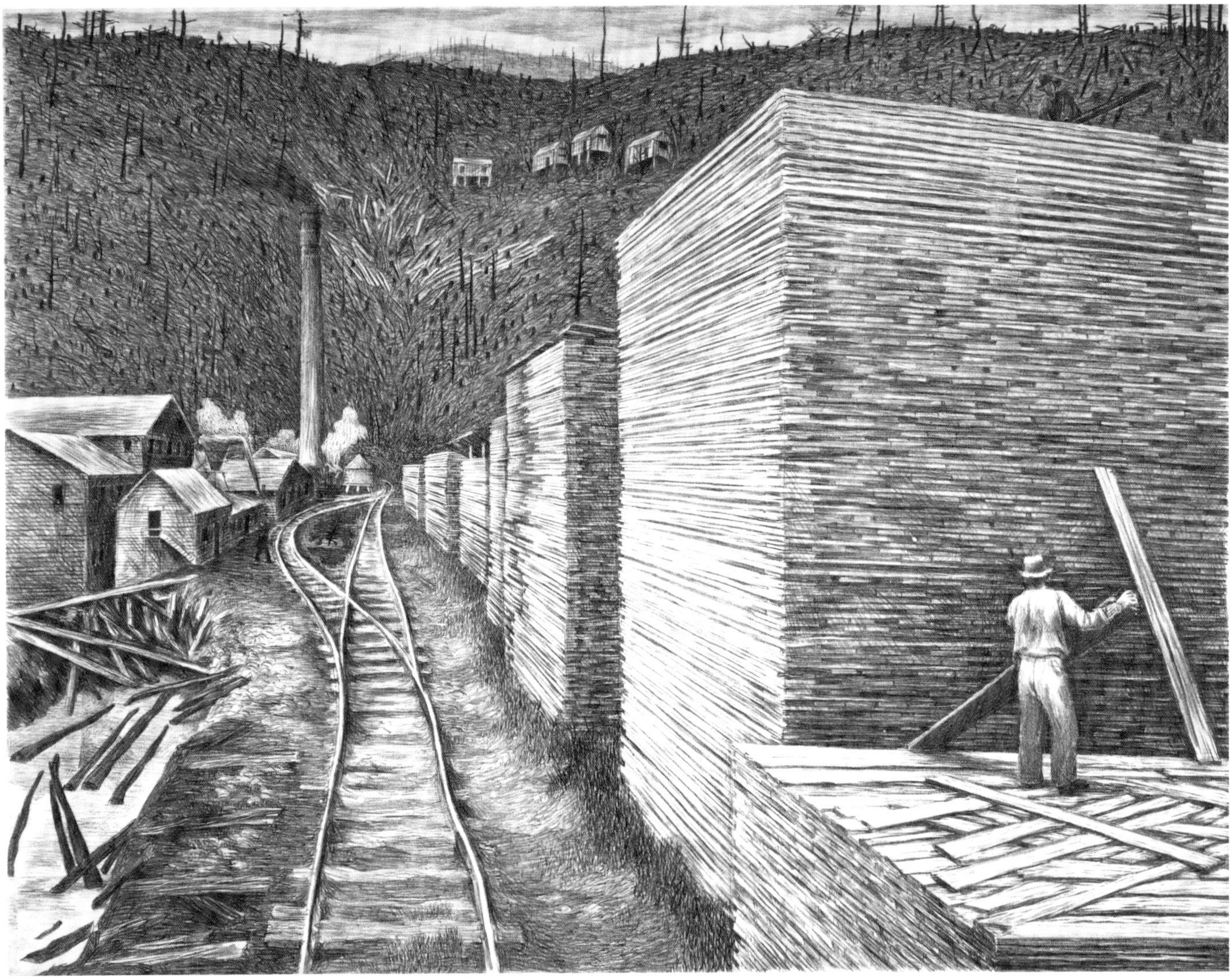

42
Bernarda Bryson Shahn
American, 1903–2004
Cut-Over Land (Timberland), from the *Resettlement* Series, 1935
Lithograph on ivory wove paper, 9 5/8 × 12 1/2

43
William Sharp
American, 1900–1961
Art Fair, 1940
Etching and aquatint on cream wove paper, 10 15/16 × 8 7/8

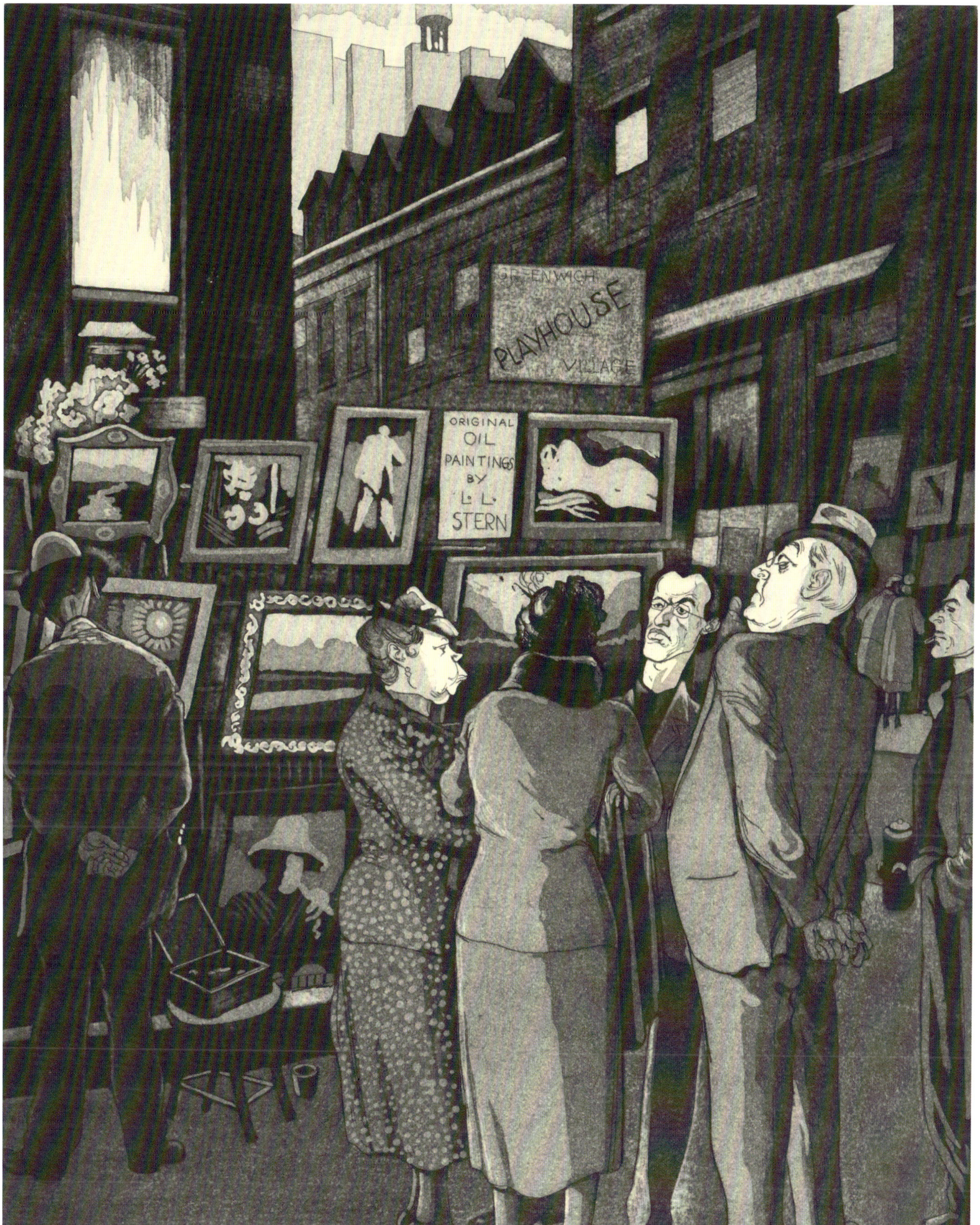
GREENWICH
PLAYHOUSE
VILLAGE
ORIGINAL
OIL
PAINTINGS
BY
L. L.
STERN

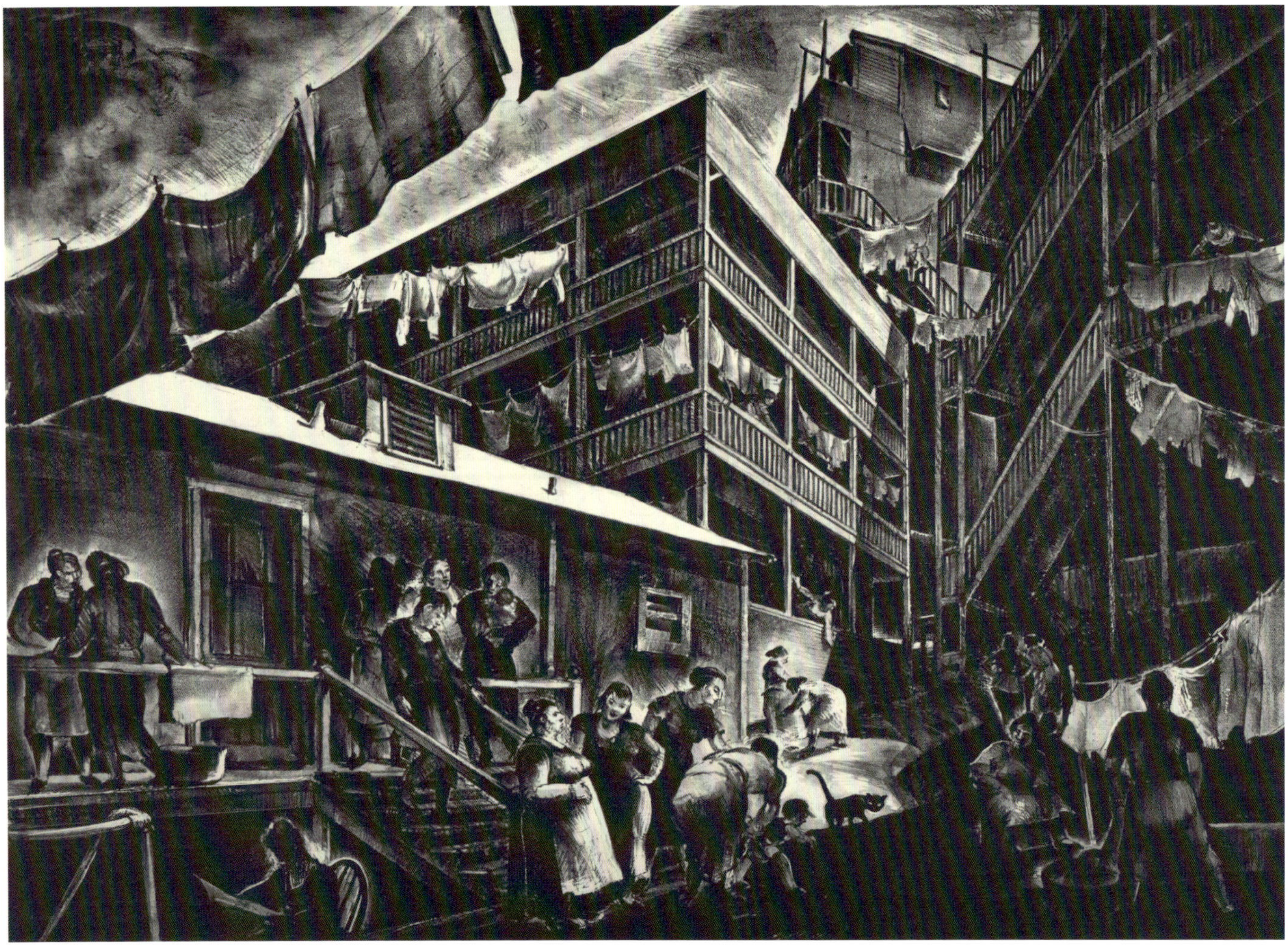

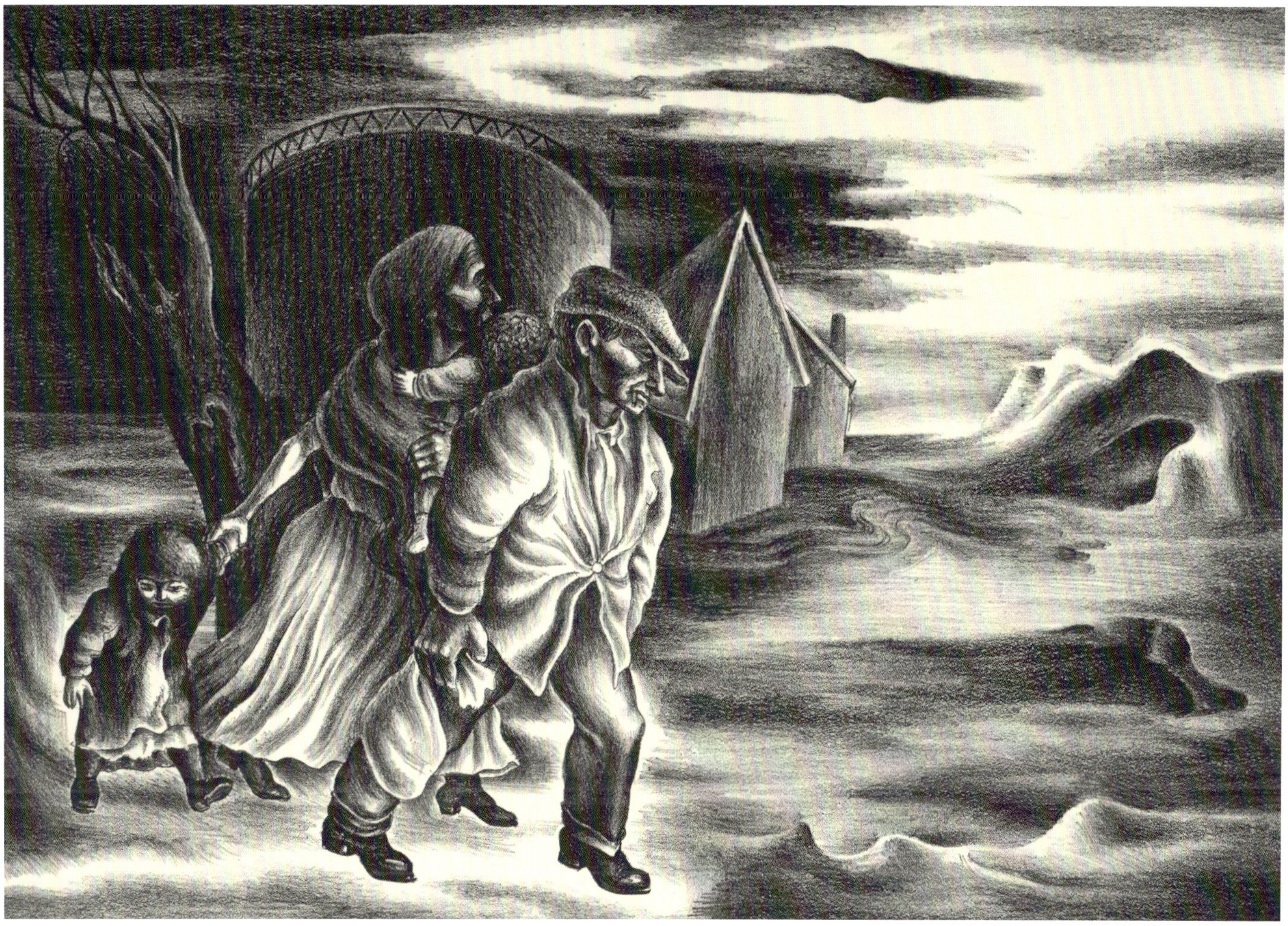

44

Millard Owen Sheets

American, 1907–1989

Family Flats, 1935

Lithograph on cream wove paper,

15¾ x 22

45

Mitchell Siporin

American, 1910–1976

The Family, date unknown

Lithograph on cream wove paper,

9 x 13

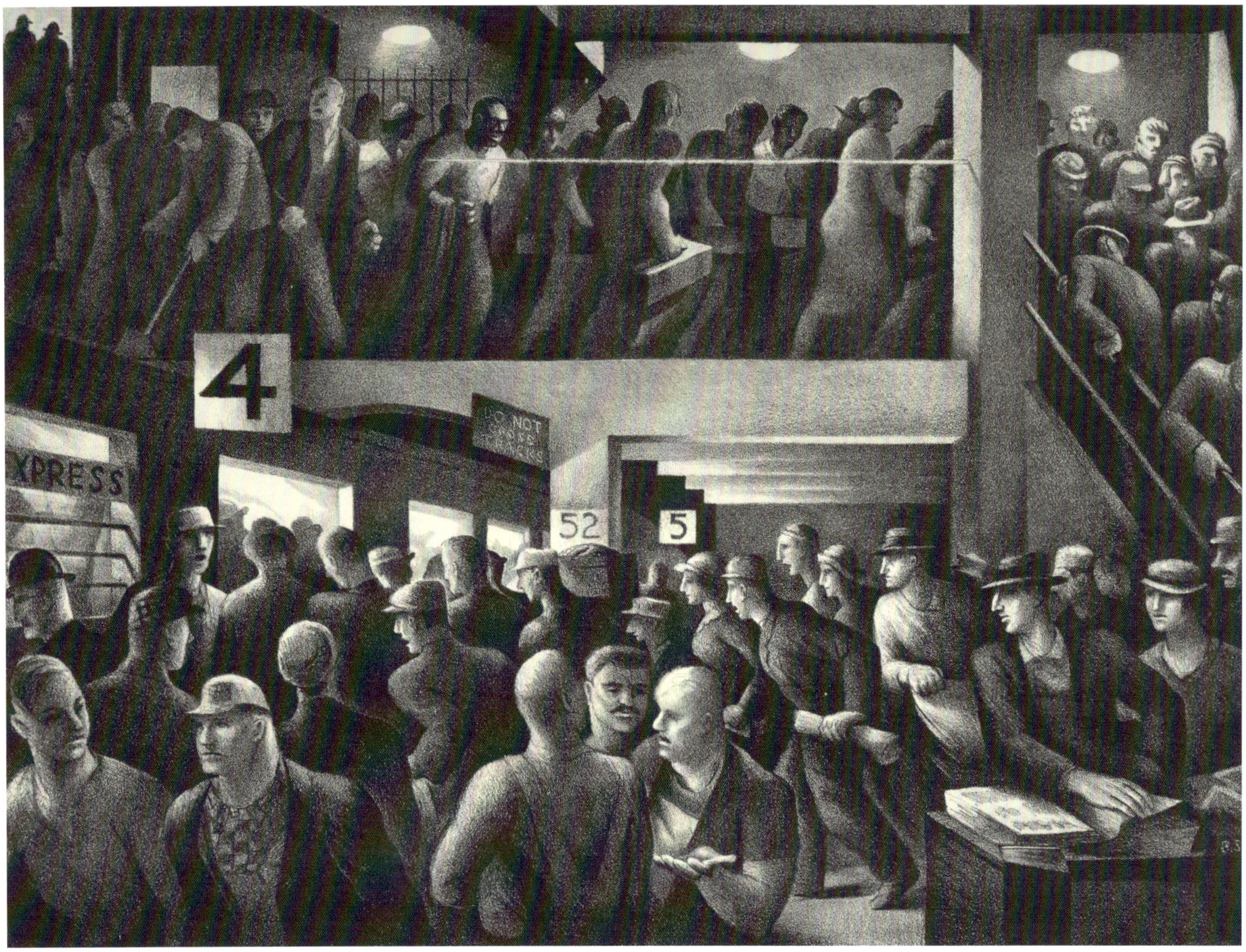

46
Benton Spruance
American, 1904–1967
The People Work: Morning, 1936
Lithograph on cream wove paper,
$13\frac{11}{16} \times 18\frac{7}{8}$

47
Bernard Steffen
American, 1907–1980
Hoeing, date unknown
Screenprint on cream wove paper,
$10\frac{7}{8} \times 13\frac{7}{8}$

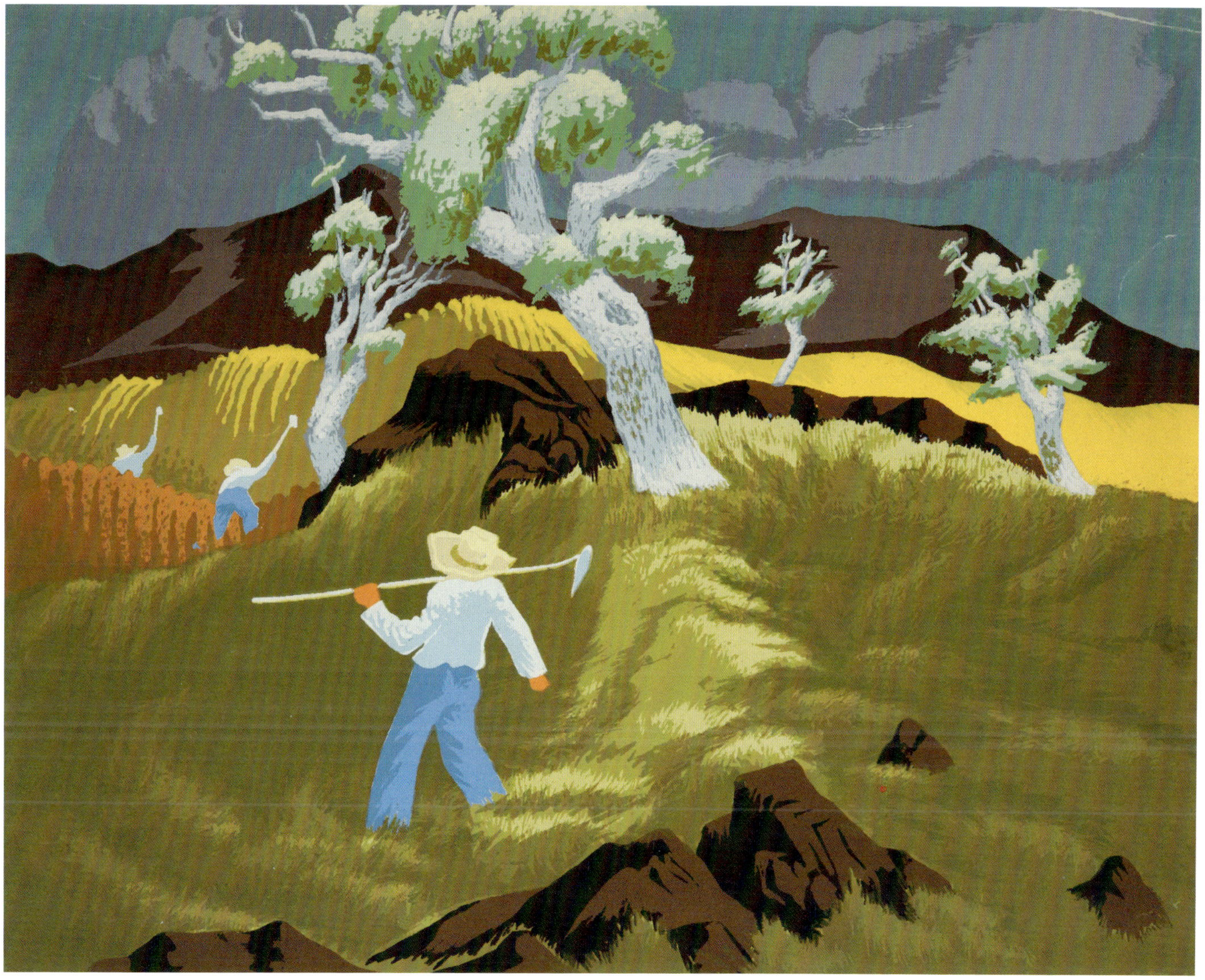

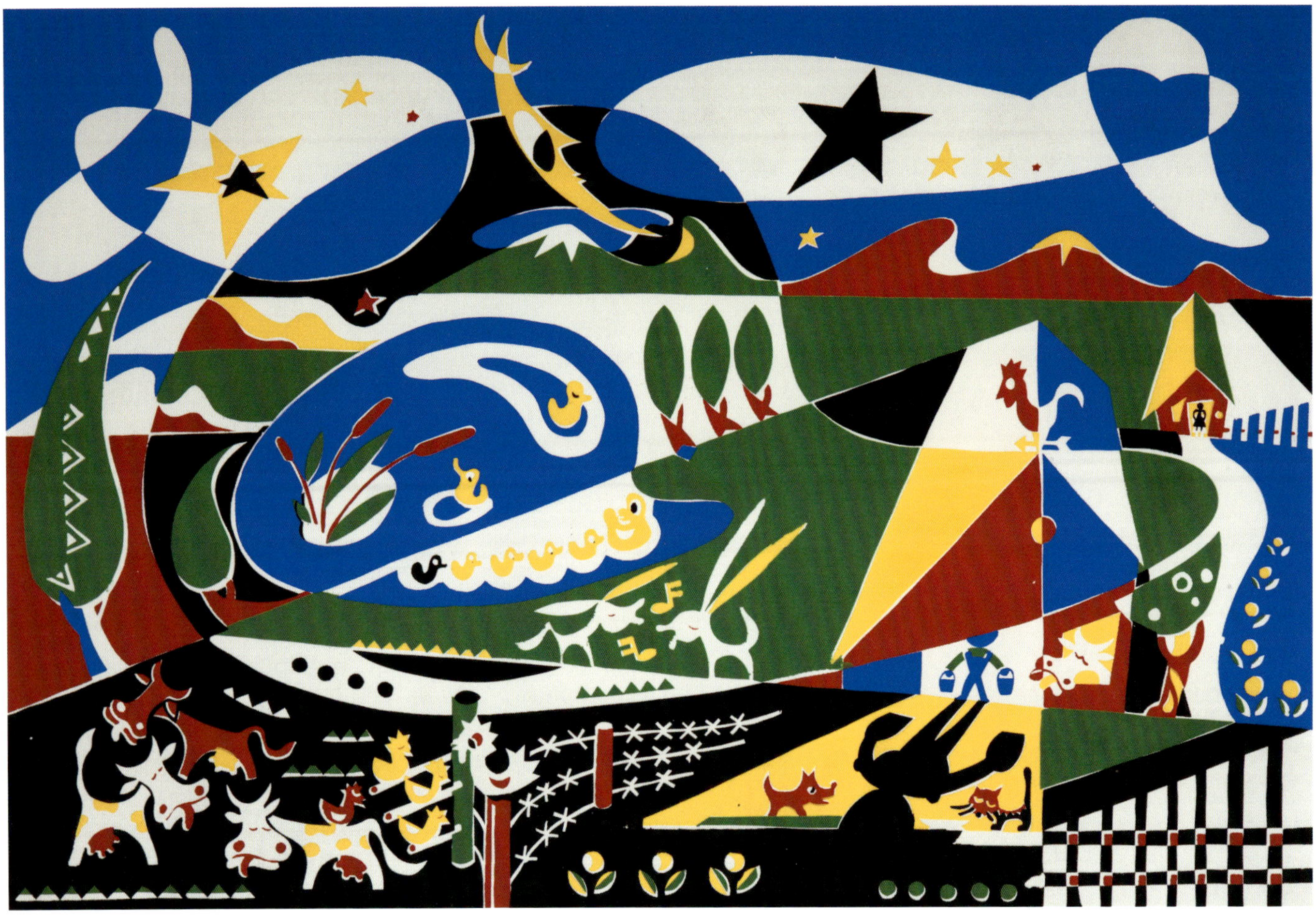

48

John F. Stenvall

American, 1907–1988

Farm at Night, 1940

Color screenprint on cream paper, 12 × 18

49

Harry Sternberg

American, 1904–2001

Steel Mills (Smoke Stacks), 1937

Screenprint on paper, $10\frac{3}{8} \times 14\frac{1}{16}$

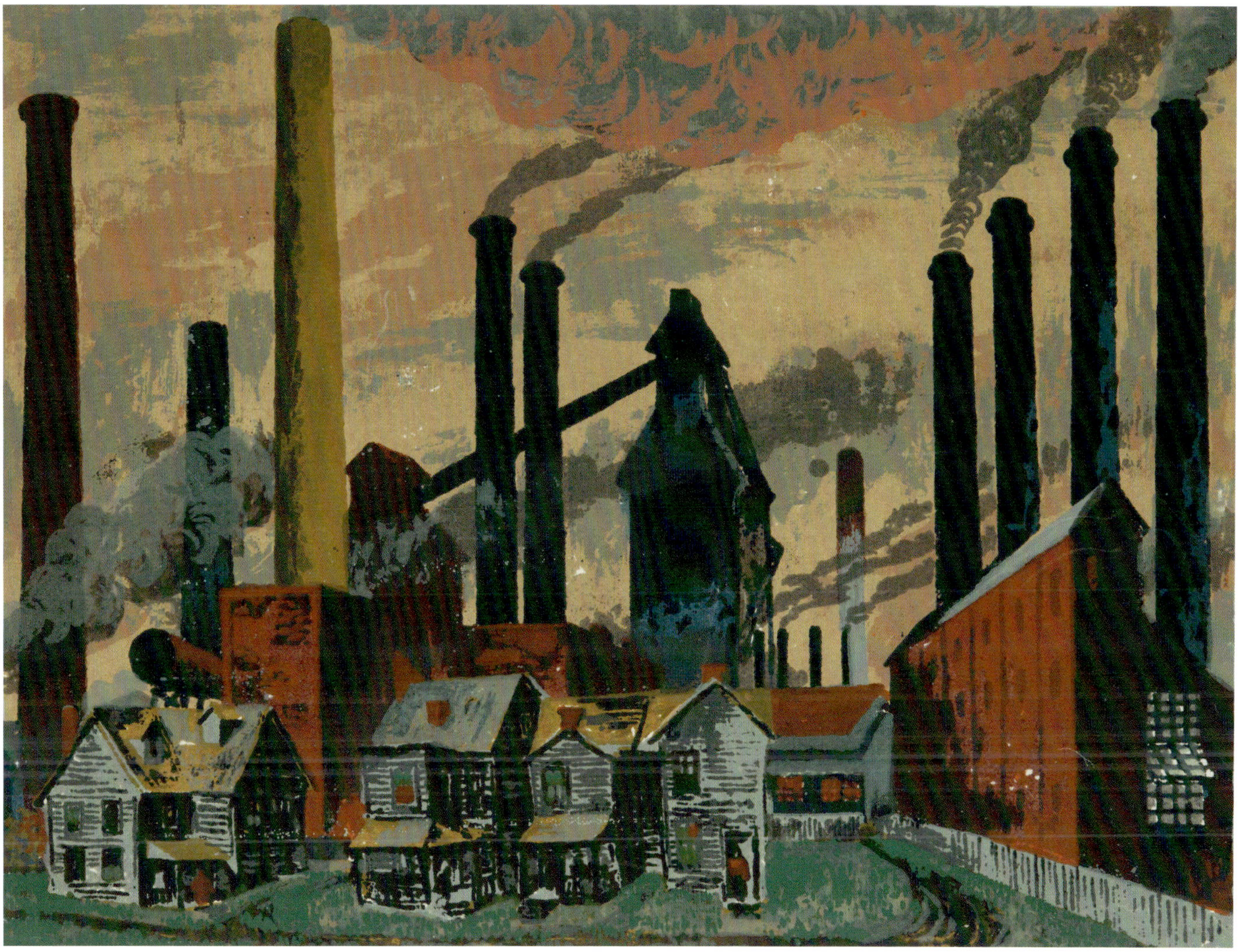

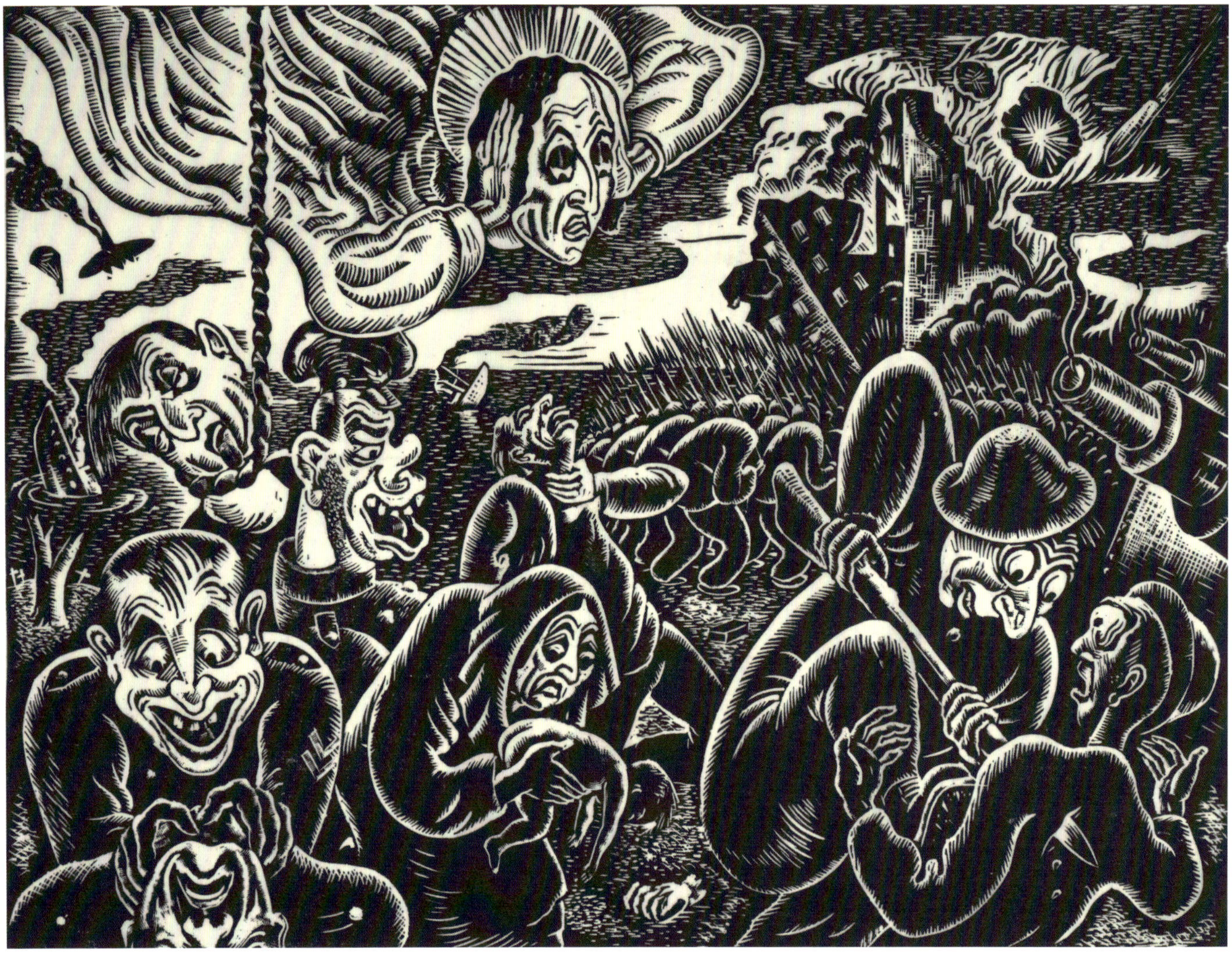

50
Charles Surendorf
American, 1906–1979
God Comes Down to Inspect
His Creations, 1941
Woodcut on cream japan paper,
9 × 12 1/16

51
Charles Turzak
American, 1899–1985
Chicago River, 1930
Woodcut, 11 1/4 × 9 1/4

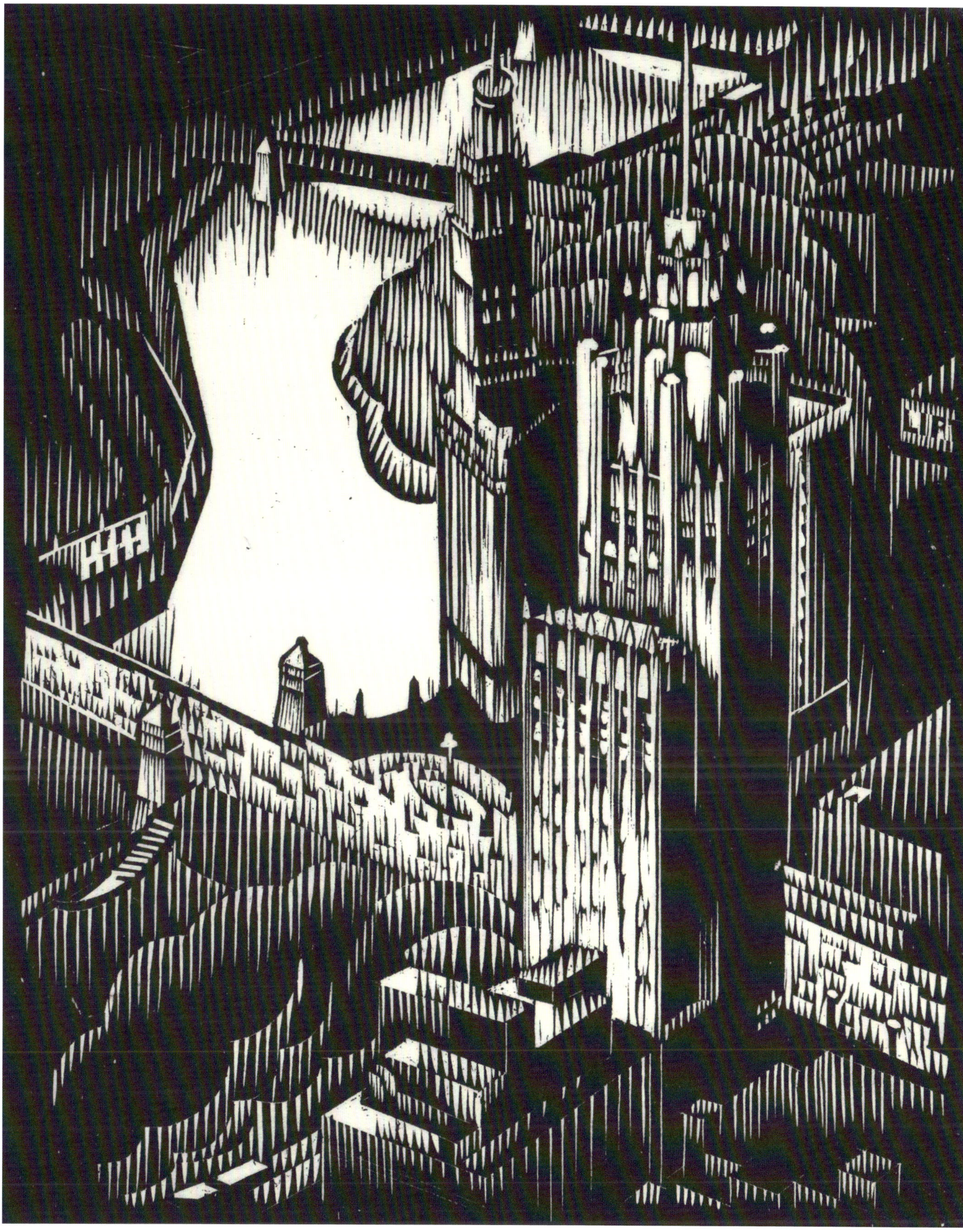

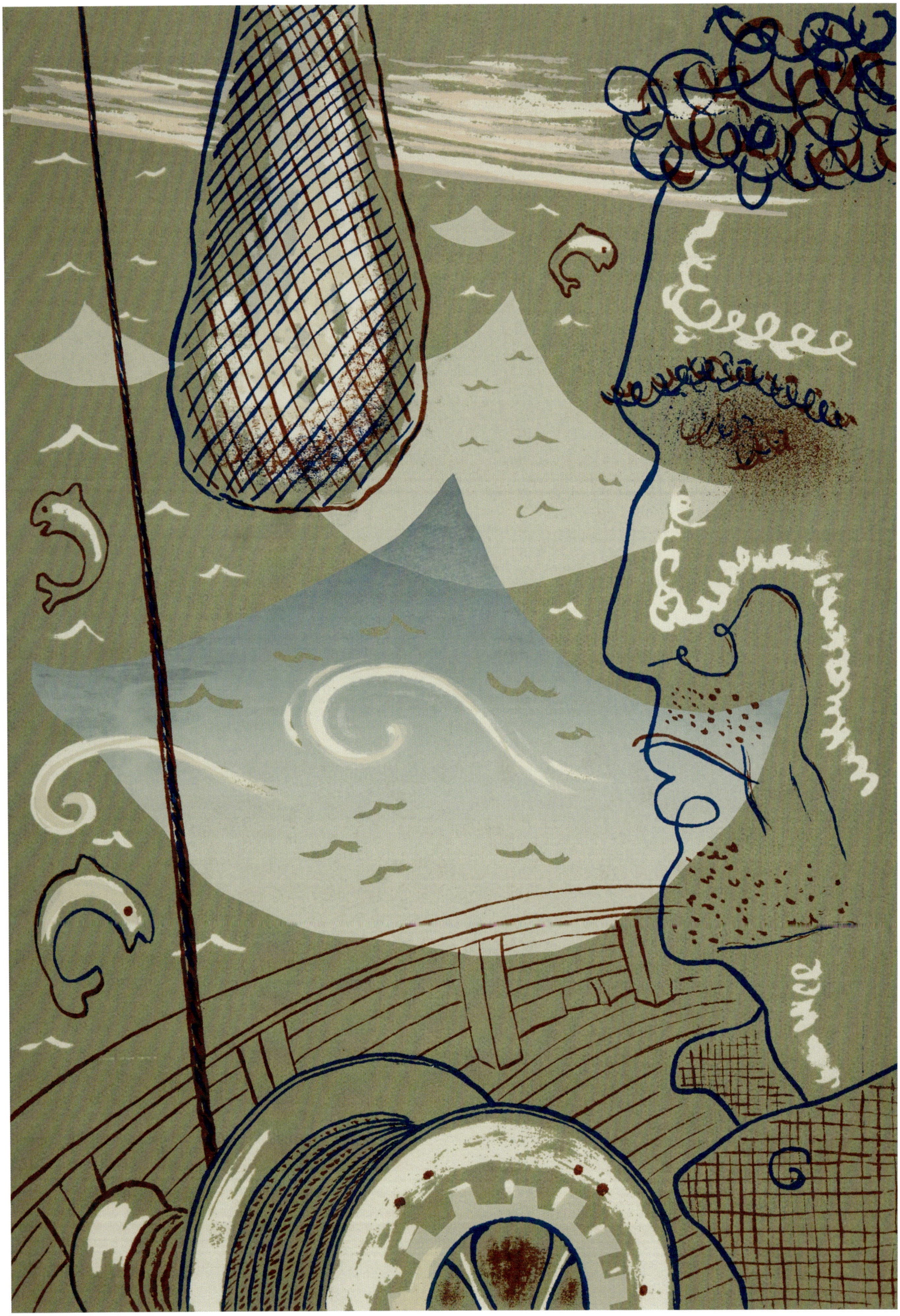

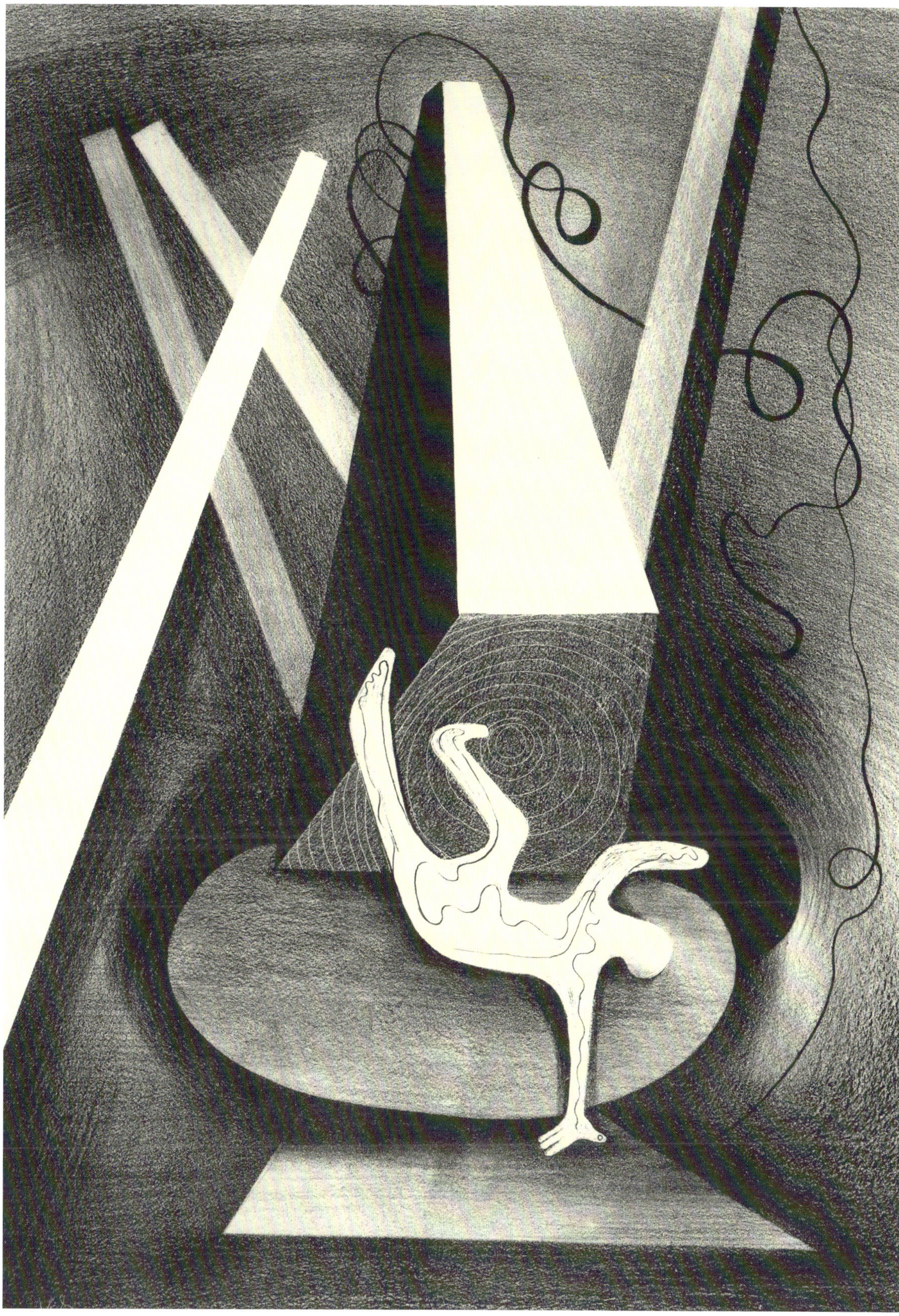

52
Anthony Velonis
American, 1911–1997
Half-Ton Fish, 1938
Color screenprint on cream wove paper, 20 1/16 × 14

53
Herman Volz
American, 1904–1990
Industrial Accident, 1940
Lithograph on cream wove paper, 17 1/16 × 12 1/4

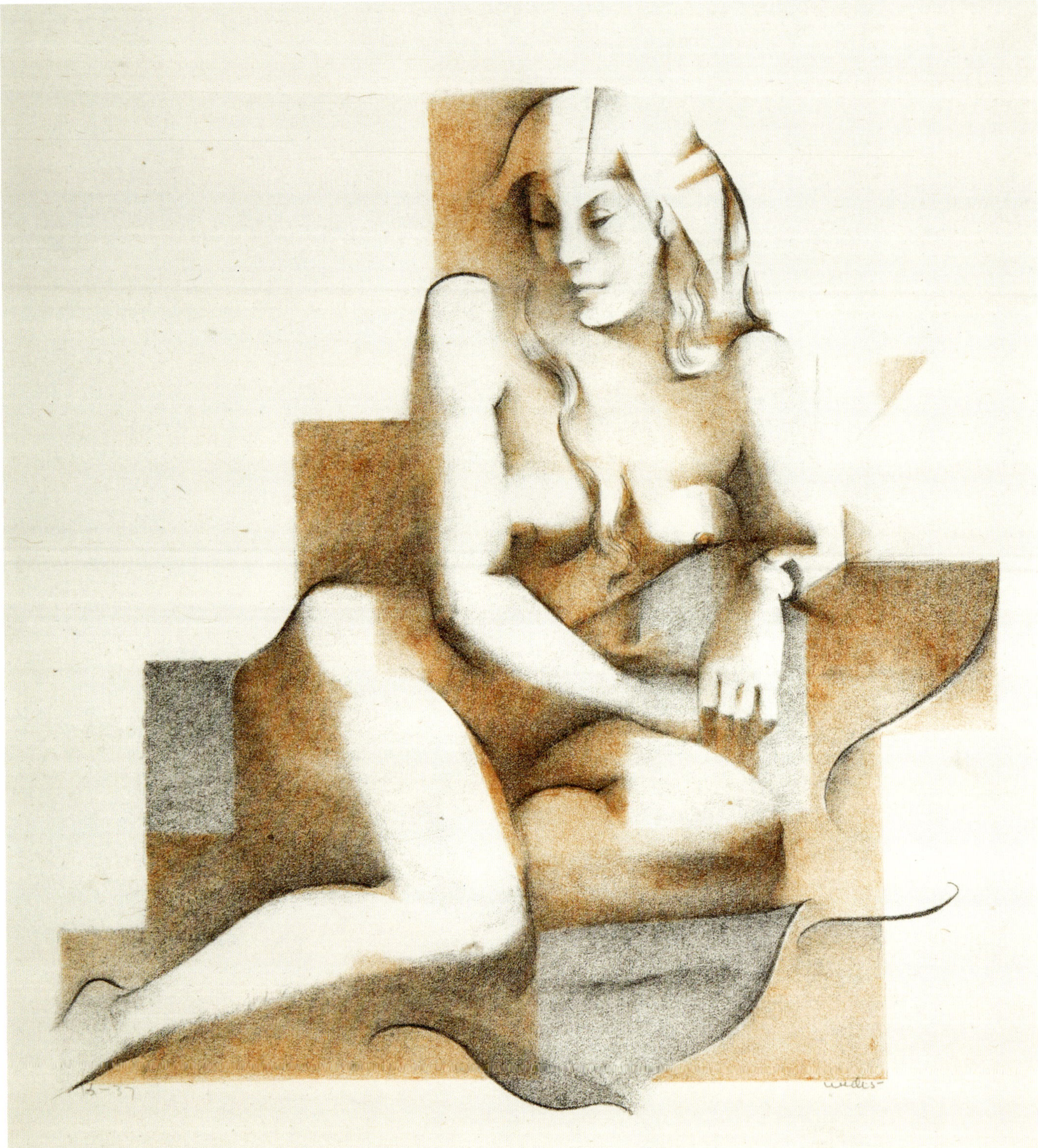

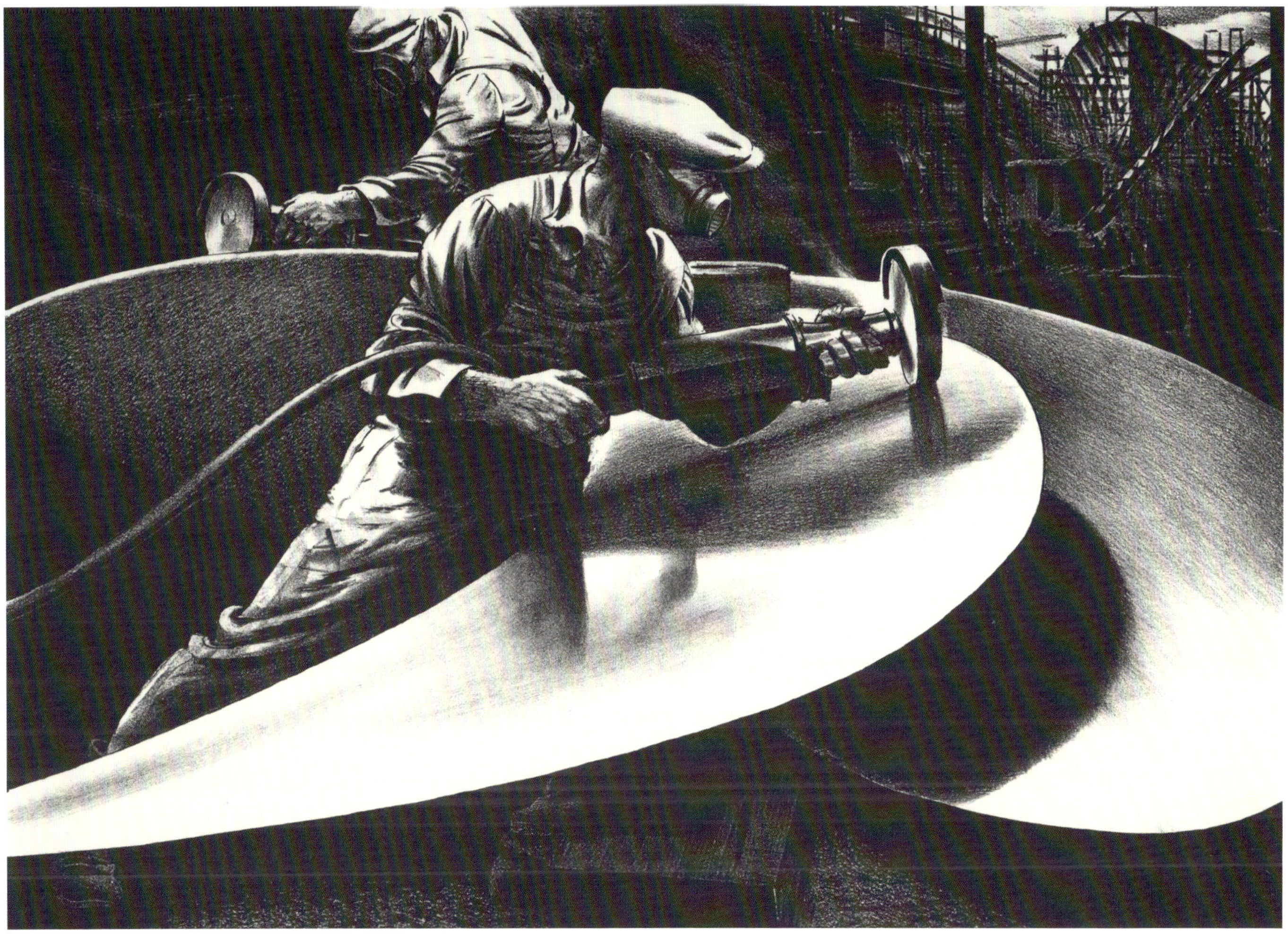

54
Kaye Waters
American, 1906–1955
Nude 5, 1937
Color lithograph on ivory laid paper,
10 1/16 × 9

55
Edward Arthur Wilson
American, 1886–1970
Untitled (Sanding the Propeller), 1941
Lithograph on ivory wove paper,
9 × 12 7/8

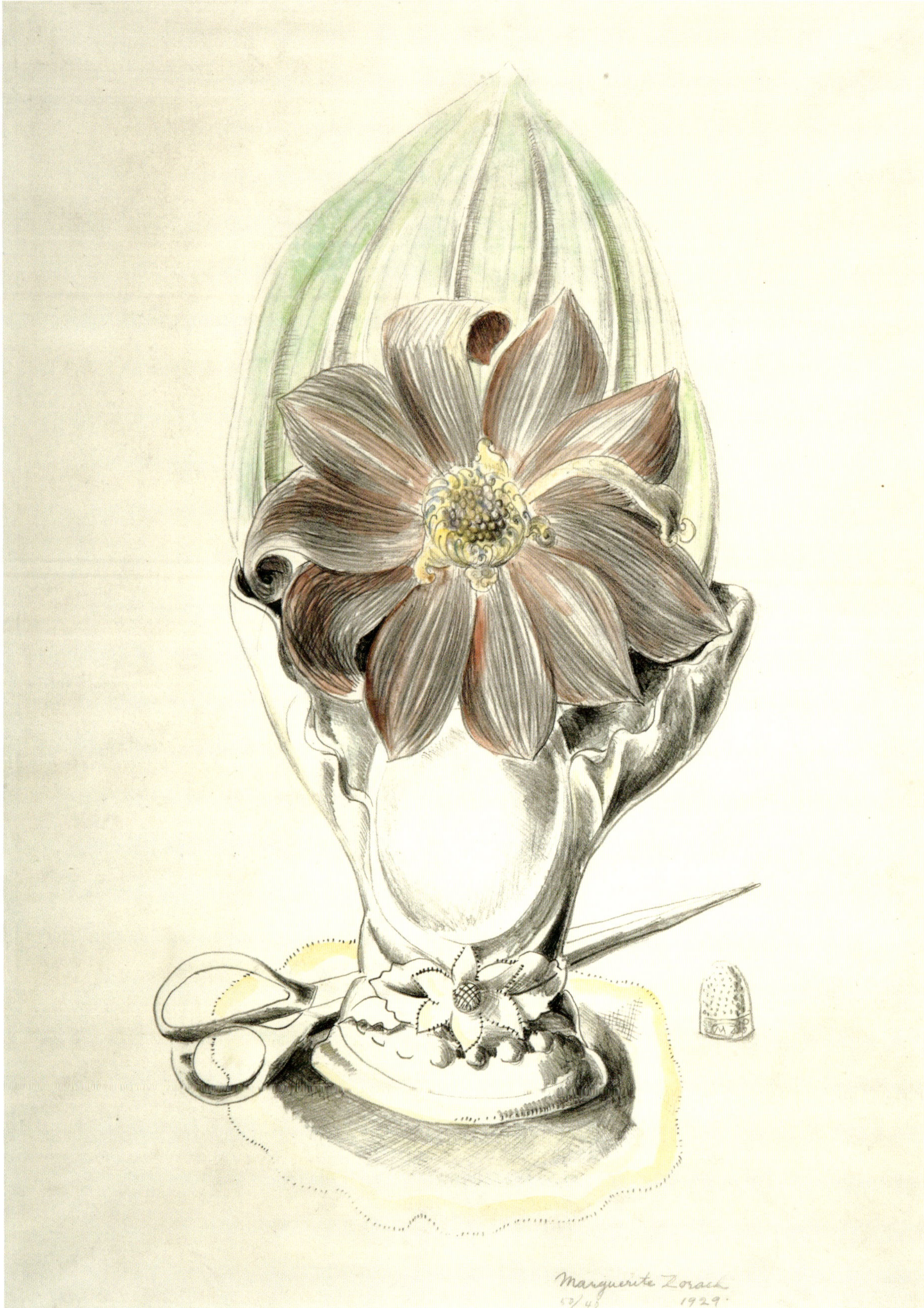

56
Marguerite Zorach
American, 1887–1968
Untitled (Autumn color flower still life), 1929
Lithograph and watercolor, 16½ x 12

DePaul Art Museum staff

Louise Lincoln
Director

Laura Fatemi
Associate Director

Gregory Harris
Assistant Curator

Alison Kleiman
Administrative Assistant

Celia DeBoer
Administrative Assistant

Jenny Cotto
Building Maintenance

Interns
Makenzi Fricker
Amy Kellenberger
Nik Massey

This publication was edited by
Susan Davidson and designed by
Roy Brooks of Fold Four, Inc.